"Who knew Black Sabbath could be mined for such theological gems! Jack Holloway makes connections I would have missed, and the result is a stellar exploration of theology Black Sabbath style! Fantastic read!"

—Thomas Jay Oord, Northwind Theological Seminary

"Jack Holloway clearly knows his way around both metal music and radical Christianity. Readers of this book will hear, feel, and, most of all, *live* the uplifting spiritual experiences that Holloway finds in the terrifying music of Black Sabbath. *Hands of Doom* is a hell of a book in every way."

—Gregory Erickson, New York University

"Jack Holloway's powerful book is a call to revolutionary justice. He traces a theological thread through Black Sabbath's music that begins with doom and ends with a call to radical application of the only force that can possibly address the fear and upheaval of our times: yes, this book about Black Sabbath is ultimately a book about love. Brimming with insight and innate musicality, *Hands of Doom* is an essential guide to the true meaning of faith."

—Elizabeth M. Edman, author of *Queer Virtue: What LGBTQ People Know about Life and Love and How It Can Revitalize Christianity*

"The black clothes, the upside-down crucifixes, the bat—it's strange to think that Black Sabbath can have anything to say about theology, and yet Jack Holloway brilliantly explains how this seminal heavy metal band illuminates divinity, precisely because they took the darkness as seriously as the light. An incantatory elucidation of an overlooked aspect of a group that changed rock music forever, and a devilishly delightful reading of pop culture's transcendent appeal."

—**Ed Simon**, author of *Pandemonium: A Visual History of Demonology*

"To read Jack Holloway's theological account on the music of Black Sabbath was to discover a treasure I never thought existed. This poetic and vibrant book carries a theology of gloom and doom that can take us away from the often wishy-washy notions of hope within Christianity, and into places of transformation. . . . More than ever, we need art that makes us imagine a new world. In this absolutely brilliant book, Holloway shows us musical ways to do it."

—**Cláudio Carvalhaes**, Union Theological Seminary

Hands of Doom

Short Theological Engagements with Popular Music

Series Editor: Christian Scharen

Editorial Committee: Margarita Simon Guillory, Jeff Keuss, Mary McDonough, Myles Werntz, Daniel White Hodge

Short Theological Engagements with Popular Music features theologians who have a passion for particular popular artists and who offer robust theological engagements with the work of that artist—engaging a song, an album, or a whole body of work over a career. Books in the series are accessible, yet deep both in their theological and musical engagement. Each book foregrounds ideas of interest in the musician's work, first, and puts these into conversation with the context and culture, second, and the Christian tradition, third. Each book, therefore, includes analysis of the cultural artifact, cultural context, and the relation to Christian tradition. Each book endeavors, as well, to speak with vitality to the challenges of living with God's mercy and justice in today's world.

Hands of Doom

The Apocalyptic Imagination of
BLACK SABBATH

Jack Holloway

 CASCADE *Books* · Eugene, Oregon

HANDS OF DOOM
The Apocalyptic Imagination of Black Sabbath

Short Theological Engagements with Popular Music

Cascade Books
An Imprint of Wipf and Stock Publishers
199 W. 8th Ave., Suite 3
Eugene, OR 97401

www.wipfandstock.com

PAPERBACK ISBN: 978-1-6667-3403-4
HARDCOVER ISBN: 978-1-6667-2945-0
EBOOK ISBN: 978-1-6667-2946-7

Cataloguing-in-Publication data:

Names: Holloway, Jack, author.

Title: Hands of doom : the apocalyptic imagination of Black Sabbath / by Jack Holloway.

Description: Eugene, OR: Cascade Books, 2022 | Series: Short Theological Engagements with Popular Music | Includes bibliographical references.

Identifiers: ISBN 978-1-6667-3403-4 (paperback) | ISBN 978-1-6667-2945-0 (hardcover) | ISBN 978-1-6667-2946-7 (ebook)

Subjects: LCSH: Black Sabbath (Musical group). | Heavy metal (Music)—History and criticism. | Apocalypse in music. | Popular music—Religious aspects.

Classification: LCC ML421.B57 H65 2022 (print) | LCC ML421.B57 (ebook)

06/14/22

Contents

𝔄𝔠𝔨𝔫𝔬𝔴𝔩𝔢𝔡𝔤𝔪𝔢𝔫𝔱𝔰

T his project would not have been possible were it not for the prompting and guidance of Christian Scharen, to whom I am eternally grateful. I must also thank: my wife, Debbie, who encouraged, inspired, and cared for me, challenged me intellectually and literarily, and also edited several portions of this book; the many friends who helped me think through and research the subject matter, and who read early drafts of different chapters—Chris Matthews, Zach Minuto, Nicole Renna, Matt Dean, Ethan Johnson, Joel Avery, Tommy Von Voigt, Hallie Stotler, Nico Márquez, Colin Weiss, and Matt Brake; my professors William Lyons and Esther Hamori for motivating and educating me on prophetic, apocalyptic, and wisdom literature of the ancient Near East; and my bandmates, Marc Remache, Shahob Newman, Dylan DeFeo, and Siena Vaccara, who inspire me musically and have given me the opportunity to play Sabbath songs live.

Finally, a special thanks for the lives and work of Joseph Blenkinsopp, Terence Fretheim, Norman Gottwald, Rosemary Radford Reuther, and Greg Tate. May they rest in peace.

Abbreviations

ABD   *Anchor Bible Dictionary*

EAAH   *Encyclopedia of African American History*

GEP   *Gale Encyclopedia of Psychology*

NAAAL   *Norton Anthology of African American Literature*

ODPF   *Oxford Dictionary of Phrase and Fable*

OTP   *Old Testament Pseudepigrapha*

TWOT   *Theological Wordbook of the Old Testament*

1

Introduction

The 1960s was a decade brimming with hopes of revolution, an electric time for a zealous counterculture. The Vietnam War loomed in the background, a fraught international situation that fueled the counterculture's pursuit of radical societal transformation. But 1969 would prove to be a decisive year, as the tide was turned by a wholly other spirit. Richard Nixon took office in January, the Manson murders took place in August, and in December a man was shot and killed at a Rolling Stones concert at the Altamont Speedway in northern California.

Equipped with images of Manson's long-haired "hippie" cult of killers, Nixon's administration and their so-called silent majority was determined to crush all opponents of status quo tranquility. Medgar Evers had been assassinated in '63, President John F. Kennedy in '64, Malcolm X in '65, Martin Luther King Jr. and presidential hopeful Robert Kennedy in '68, and in December of '69 the Black Panther Fred Hampton was assassinated by the FBI. Americans could turn on their television sets to see cops beating up protesters in 1968. A year later, self-proclaimed revolutionaries rioted for four days in Chicago in the "Days of Rage." Also in '69, Nixon authorized Operation Menu, a relentless carpet bombing of Cambodia, which brought immeasurable death and destruction to Southeast Asia. It was not only cultural upheaval that defined the 1960s, but also violent backlash.

On the one hand, groups of people all over the world saw themselves on the cusp of a beloved community which was before thought impossible. On the other hand, it became clear the more inspiring that vision of community became, the more in danger it became. Fight hard enough for social change and you will be crushed.

It is little surprise this is the precise point where a new musical genre emerges that surveys a freshly understood aspect of existence: doom. Black Sabbath played their first show on August 1969, the same month as the Manson murders. The following year, three months after Fred Hampton's assassination, Black Sabbath released their self-titled album. Its opening track, "Black Sabbath," Rob Halford of Judas Priest called "the most evil song that's ever been written."[1]

There had been songs about the devil, there had been songs about evil and hell and darkness, but there had never been music this sharply ominous. The sole purpose of this music was to give expression to horror. It was a new genre, which would eventually be aptly titled "doom metal." This new music enveloped listeners with heaviness and dread. At the opening of their flagship song, lonely bell chimes issue from the sound of thunder, and a whole reality is invoked. Here, evil is not some momentary lapse in a generally good state of affairs. These bells announce a tyranny of evil. Here is a song that could give you nightmares.

1. Newton, "Judas Priest's Rob Halford."

The world had seen countless horrors, and instead of using music to create joy and hope in the midst of suffering and despair, to shine a light where there was darkness, Black Sabbath gave expression to that very darkness. Guitarist Tony Iommi said,

> Everywhere else it was all flower power and everything nice and happy and people weren't writing about real life: wars and famine and all the other things nobody wants to face. So we saw that and thought we should be doing it.[2]

When listeners heard Sabbath's title track for the first time, they were given what they feared: an image of a world without hope, where the devil reigns and God is no more than a desperate wish. Sabbath deployed the medieval imagery of hell, but did not relegate hell to some lower realm reserved for history's worst actors. No, the bells in "Black Sabbath" announce that we are in hell. We are its desperate inhabitants pitifully crying out to God to rescue us from our fiery prison. There is nowhere to run. There is nothing left to do but cry, "Oh no, no, please God help me!" This tortured cry was given uncanny expression by lead singer Ozzy Osbourne's strange, devastating vocals. There is nothing pleasant or nice about his voice, but it is, for this reason, essential to the music.

In the 1960s, a community ready for the times to change for the better was instead rudely introduced to malevolent depths of existence. As James Baldwin wrote in 1972,

> Hope—the hope that we, human beings, can be better than we are—dies hard; perhaps one can

2. Iommi and Lammers, *Iron Man*, 82.

> no longer live if one allows that hope to die. But
> it is also hard to see what one sees.[3]

People in this period were confronted with evil in its starkest forms: senseless militarism, racial injustice, unthinkable bloodshed. The heights of prophetic imagination invoked in Dr. King's "I Have a Dream" speech, and in songs like Bob Dylan's "The Times They Are a-Changin'," were followed by the lows of irredeemable loss and relentless violence. As sociologist Deena Weinstein wrote, "The master word of the 1960s, LOVE, was negated by its binary opposite, EVIL."[4] These new depths needed a corresponding soundtrack; Black Sabbath would provide it.

The 1970s would be a different kind of decade, defined for many by a jaded, gritty outlook. The villains in horror films stopped being supernatural beings or alien monsters. Tobe Hooper, director of the 1974 film *The Texas Chainsaw Massacre*, which is still today considered by many the most horrifying movie of all time, said of the film: "Man was the real monster here."[5]

Black Sabbath were among the original foragers of this burgeoning pessimism. Their music does not provide escape from a woeful world, but rather takes us deeper into the reality of evil, a special classroom home to its own lessons that no other can teach.

Black Sabbath Today

A cultural upheaval similar to that of the 1960s is occurring today. The Black Lives Matter movement captivated the world much in the same way that the Civil Rights

3. Baldwin, *No Name in the Street*, 36.

4. Weinstein, *Heavy Metal*, 18.

5. Quoted in Bowen, "Return of the Power Tool Killer," 16.

movement and the anti-war movement did in the '60s. But something that sets this movement apart is its profoundly negative character—that is to say, the social uprising we are seeing today is almost a cynical one. In practice, it is hopeful, but—and I am speaking here from my own experience, having been a part of this movement for seven years—it harbors a biting cynicism regarding the status quo and whether it can be changed for the better.

The presidency of Barack Obama had been precipitated by a populist movement hungry for serious social transformation. But while "Yes we can," "Hope," and "Change" were Obama's winning messages, eight years of his administration did little to affect the realities of systemic racism, wealth inequality, and climate catastrophe. And we were not prepared for the wild regression to follow with the presidency of Donald Trump. Clearly a reaction to the Obama years, Trump's administration brought a shameless, anti-intellectual chauvinism to the center of public life, and exacerbated all the major crises facing the United States. Fed up with the volatility and inadequacy of change in a broken, corrupt system, more and more people have become radicalized and insistent on revolution.

I am one of these people. I want it to be clear at the outset that my own commitments are decidedly in favor of revolutionaries, and my discussions of Black Sabbath have been shaped by my charged political context and the liberationist outlook I maintain. I do not listen to music in a vacuum, nor do I separate my music listening from the momentous activity of which I am a part. I biked alongside hundreds of protesters on "Justice Rides" in New York City, and on one of the rides another biker played "War Pigs" by Black Sabbath on a Bluetooth speaker. In this time of resistance, Sabbath's music has empowered and inspired me and others, and that experience has shaped this book. So while I dialogue with music critics and books on Black Sabbath, I also engage other conversation partners, like black liberationists, revolutionaries, critical theorists, as well as modern theologians, feminists, and biblical scholars. Some may object that I veer off the subject of Black Sabbath and stray into "politics." To this I can only say, Black Sabbath is not apolitical, nor is writing a book apolitical.

I am not alone in my experience. I am one player in a larger movement of metalheads seeking to raise consciousness in the metal scene. In April 2020, the Pittsburgh hardcore band Killer of Sheep designed a Black Lives Matter T-shirt using Black Sabbath's signature Master of Reality font. Black Sabbath then mass-produced their own T-shirts with the same design, donating 100 percent of the proceeds to the Black Lives Matter Global Network, a fundraiser that continues to this day.[6] Black Sabbath fans found inspiration for their anti-fascism in Black Sabbath's music, and in turn influenced the band to update its own anti-fascist stance. This interaction is shaping the future of metal, which for decades has been in need of an exorcism of the forces of racism, sexism, and xenophobia.

Sabbath's music has also become more prescient in light of the climate crisis we face today. My generation was born just in time to witness the disintegration of the earth's environment. Images of hellfire and damnation carry a whole new resonance now that we have seen, for example, whole areas of California engulfed in flames so that the sky turned red.[7] Nothing I was taught in school, in church, at home, or on television prepared me for that vision. The Great Barrier Reef is dying.[8] The Gulf Stream is nearing collapse.[9]

6. Kelly, "Inside Heavy Metal's Battle against White Supremacy."
7. Rubenstein and Cabanatuan, "Bay Area Transfixed."
8. Cave, "Great Barrier Reef."
9. Carrington, "Climate Crisis."

The climate I knew as a kid is being drastically altered. The distinctions between the seasons of spring, summer, fall, winter, which have been attested to throughout human history, are becoming meaningless as the climate is becoming more extreme. Venice, a destination reflected in thousands of pages of history books and European literature, is flooding and already becoming uninhabitable.[10] The same will be true for countless other places. The world I will inhabit when my hair is gray will hardly resemble the world as it was when I was born.

All the while, the ultra-rich, corporate heads, and governmental officials all over the world are not taking the crisis as seriously as they absolutely should given the gravity of the situation. And we are nearing a point of no return.

My generation has been forced to face the fact that, because of human indifference, human overreach, and human recklessness, the earth as we have known it is doomed. We have had to confront and reconcile ourselves with a planet that is growing increasingly volatile and disastrous. In this context, Black Sabbath's criticism of "sorcerers of madness" who bring death and destruction to the earth, as well as their sense of dread concerning the fate of the world, make their music strikingly resonant. The band itself came out of an area of the United Kingdom that was shaped in large part by the industrial revolution, laying the groundwork for the aggressive pollution of the earth we see today.

Now is the perfect time to revisit Black Sabbath, a band forged in the revolutionary counterculture of the 1960s, and on the vanguard of a grittier liberationist outlook in the early 1970s. We encounter in Geezer Butler's lyrics an unflinching pessimism, and yet also serious theological imagination. Black Sabbath might seem to surrender hope at the gates of hell, but they nonetheless laugh victoriously with a

10. Barry, "Climate Change Drives Venice Flooding."

knowing, transcendent imagination. Hidden in their satanic imagery, their cynical contempt, and their ominous proclamations is a theology of divine judgment and promise, resistant to indifference and the temptations of escapism. Black Sabbath's theology is both worldly and otherworldly, hellish and heavenly. Theirs is a negative hope, a critical idealism, which points to the brokenness of the status quo, and beyond to the heights of justice and love.

In this work, I have been greatly dependent on the exceptional and deeply theological lyrics of Geezer Butler, who wrote most of the songs discussed in this book. Guitarist Tony Iommi referred to Geezer in his autobiography as "the intelligent one," and his lyrics confirm this statement.[11] Were it not for Geezer, this book would not have been possible. He was to the band's theology what Iommi was to the music—its chief driving force.

Terence Michael Joseph "Geezer" Butler was born in July 1947. He was raised in Birmingham, UK, by Irish Catholic parents.[12] His early life was shaped by working-class poverty, the omnipresence of factories in Birmingham, and the ominous presence of bombed-out buildings after the area had suffered countless blows from enemy bombers in World War II. Geezer's brothers were drafted into the army, and expressed to him their hatred of military life. He was sure he would also be drafted, but luckily for him Britain discontinued the draft in 1963 when he was sixteen. Geezer was a serious, reflective kid, zealously devoting himself to Catholicism at a young age. But when

11. Iommi and Lammers, *Iron Man*, 74.

12. For Geezer's biography, see Wall, *Black Sabbath*; Rosen, *Wheels of Confusion*; Hoskyns, *Into the Void*; Reesman, "Geezer Butler"; Polcaro, "Sabbath's Geezer Butler"; Sharma, "Geezer Butler"; Blaine, "Gospel according to Black Sabbath"; Aarons, "Geezer Butler"; as well as Geezer's website, www.geezerbutler.com/about.

he witnessed missionaries preaching fire and brimstone, he was disillusioned by religion, seeing it as a form of social control, and began studying Satan and the occult to get away from the dogmatism he found in the church.

In his teenage years, Geezer followed the Beatles into hippie culture, growing his hair out long, wearing colorful clothes, and dropping LSD. While Ozzy and Tony were influenced by the more aggressive forms of British youth culture, like the Teds and the Mods, Geezer was more peaceful and intellectual. He became a vegan at age twenty and remains one to this day. He is a passionate animal rights activist, and uses his platform to promote organizations like PETA, Kitten Rescue, and Ace of Hearts. His experiences growing up poor, Irish, and Catholic in a war-torn English city set the coordinates for the unique theological vision he would offer in his lyrics.

While I pay close attention to Geezer's lyrics, I also discuss how Sabbath's music itself is theological, as well as the social, political, and philosophical issues that heavy metal culture raises. I am (mostly) limiting myself to the first six Sabbath albums, which constitute the highly prosperous first Ozzy period, from 1969 to 1975. These albums include *Black Sabbath*, *Paranoid*, *Master of Reality*, *Vol. 4*, *Sabbath Bloody Sabbath*, and *Sabotage*. While I occasionally discuss later Sabbath work, they simply have too much material for me to go beyond these monumental albums for the present study.

Black Sabbath's albums harbor a wealth of theological material, offering rich insight and honest struggle. My purpose for this book is to explore that rich material and mine for theological insights. In chapter 1, I compare Sabbath songs to biblical lament, and discuss the theme of mental illness in Sabbath's music, as well as their unique view of drug use in the soul's quest for relief of mental anguish. In chapter 2, I outline Sabbath's apocalyptic imagination, comparing their witness to the prophets and the apocalyptic literature of the Bible. In chapter 3, I dig into Sabbath's anticapitalism, and their critique of caste society. In chapter 4, I address the history behind Sabbath's music, tracing the development of the blues in the African American experience and its reception by British musicians, and I wrestle with the ethical questions this history brings up. In chapter 5, I take a look at the elusive figure of Satan in Sabbath's music, comparing and contrasting with the biblical depictions of Satan, and rethinking Satanology for a postmodern context. In chapter 6, I explore the theme of disillusionment at the heart of Sabbath's music, searching for a theology against illusions. Finally, in chapter 7, I tackle Sabbath's theology of love, and how it squares with their seeming misanthropy and sense of doom. Throughout, my purpose will not be to relate or liken Sabbath to this or that theology. Rather, I will mine Sabbath's music, lyrics, and context and present it as a theological vision in its own right. Black Sabbath will be my sacred text, and like musicians riff on the melody, I will riff on Sabbath's ideas.

What Is Theology?

This book is for Black Sabbath fans, but it is also a theology book. I do not know many metalheads who read theology books, so a word about what theology is is in order. Theology is the study of God, but the word itself seems like a non sequitur, as it begs the question of God. Is God not—at least, generally—silent and invisible? How do we study something we cannot hear or see? Theology, it may seem, should rather be the study of what humans have believed about God, said about God, and done in the name of God. But the theologian wants to do more than that. The theologian wants to make truthful statements about God as a reality.

In this pursuit, people like myself see two essential relating factors at play in theology: an intimate connection to humanity and the earth, and a mysterious sense of otherness—immanence and transcendence, to use the theological words. God has a special relationship to humans because only humans share the idea of God. God is not an object we encounter in the world with our senses, like animals and plants, but God is nonetheless an object of thought and experience for humans. God has occurred to humans, so we cannot talk about God without talking about the humans talking about God. And yet, permeating the idea of God is what the rabbi Abraham Joshua Heschel called "the sense of the ineffable."[13] To say "God" is to invoke deep mystery and boundlessness. God occurs to the human mind as a question mark over the human order, and opens up the mind to the reality of otherness and alternative possibilities. Theology is driven by these questions of the humanity of God and what it means that God is divine.

Since we cannot talk about God without talking about the humans who are talking, we cannot talk about Black Sabbath's theology without discussing the members of the band and their historical context. Much of this book might seem more like sociology or critical theory than theology, but that is because I believe the work of theology must involve a thorough awareness of history and society.[14] History and society are inseparable from reality, and

13. Heschel, *God in Search of Man*, 65.

14. The philosopher Ludwig Feuerbach wrote that people who study humanity are in a better position to execute the task of theology than theologians because they are committed to objective reality and can observe human connections in theology. See Feuerbach, *Essence of Christianity*, 13, 89.

a theology divorced from reality is divorced from truth, and thereby God as well.

Theology is also intimately related to the experience of pain, and concern for those who are suffering and in need. In the book of Exodus, one of the first things we learn about God is that God hears the cries of Israelites enslaved in Egypt (Exodus 2:23–25). Pain cannot help but witness to the truth.[15] As long as one does not feel or hear suffering, one can entertain all manner of worldviews, ideologies, and fantasies, one can pontificate imaginatively in a hundred directions. But one who suffers pain bears the truth as a burden, is confronted with cold hard reality, and this is a privilege for which they did not ask. The experience of oppression reveals to the oppressed morality—what the world should and should not be like. For one, the world should not be like it is. The world must change, and change especially so that no one is oppressed—that is the sufferer's revelation. The sufferer is pressed beyond the present moment into a longing for a future without pain. This movement is an awakening to theological imagination. Following this emphasis on the relation between theology and suffering, I believe that insofar as Black Sabbath centers the voice of the oppressed and calls the world to radical transformation and liberation, they witness to God.

My approach to theology in this book will not involve a dependence on traditional doctrines or creeds, nor will I be justifying Black Sabbath's theology by reference to this or that biblical proof text. A theology heavy metal in character and worth its salt cannot be too systematic. The highly concentrated and not a little elitist character of

15. As the critical theorist Theodor Adorno wrote, "The need to lend a voice to suffering is a condition of all truth. For suffering is objectivity that weighs upon the subject." Adorno, *Negative Dialectics*, 17.

academic theological discourse, and the typical formulas that academic theologians adopt and prescribe, are, for the metalhead, repressive, constricting, and decisively not rock 'n' roll.

Many religious theologians will balk at the idea of a theology book about Black Sabbath—the notoriously "satanic" group that transforms good kids into morbid and irreverent misfits. The premise of this book brings up a question about the sources of theology and what counts as a sacred text. Toward this question, the feminist theologian Rosemary Radford Ruether wrote, "Systems of authority try to . . . make received symbols dictate what can be experienced as well as the interpretation of that which is experienced." As opposed to listening to and learning from real life, authoritarians try to dictate reality, even as they are thwarted by reality every step of the way. The truth is, Ruether says, "If a symbol does not speak authentically to experience, it becomes dead or must be altered to provide a new meaning."[16] This fact, contrary to what authoritarians want, is not a choice that individuals make, but rather occurs spontaneously. In one way or another, experience shapes belief.

To use an example, as a child, I believed, as was customary for all evangelical Christians in my life growing up, that if people do not make a decision to "receive Jesus Christ as your lord and savior," they are damned to eternity in hell. This belief did not survive my first year of undergraduate education, even as I attended the notoriously conservative Christian institution Regent University. To the dismay of my religious university, I simply learned too much. I did not go through any brainwashing, I did not become a hedonist or libertine, I simply took classes on various subjects, read many kinds of books, met different kinds

16. Ruether, *Sexism and God-Talk*, 12–13.

of people, and had impactful life experiences. Experience made my childhood belief in hell impossible. It strikes me today not just as profoundly absurd but actually offensive and obscene. If I can love the people destined for hell, then apparently I am more loving than God. My attitude today is, if God is a master who has created a little mouse trap where we all must confess the name "Jesus Christ" or be damned to unending torture, then God is a tyrant that we must overthrow and kill.[17]

While he was imprisoned in the 1940s for conspiring to overthrow and kill the tyrant Adolf Hitler, the German theologian Dietrich Bonhoeffer wrote, "We should find God in what we know, not in what we don't know."[18] He was arguing against a God-of-the-gaps theology which tries to find room for God by pointing to unsolved problems humans cannot explain and exploiting them to make room for theology. He believed we should not carve out a little space for God and then zealously guard that space with all our might, for doing so would mean the more we learn, the more God is on the retreat. If God is real, we should be able to find God in any place on earth, and beyond. We should be able to hear God anywhere.

Conversely, the reactionary impulse toward the modern world, Bonhoeffer wrote, is to be "sticklers for principle," who "go to war like Don Quixote against a new age."[19] Theologians today can be sticklers for principle and complain about how deviant the world has become, can turn up their noses at the Black Sabbaths and the Megan Thee Stallions and the Lil Nas Xs—or they can follow the way of Jesus. Jesus found parables of the kingdom of God in the unexpected, in common, popular experiences. To

17. See Cone, *Black Theology of Liberation*, 28, 117.

18. Bonhoeffer, *Letters and Papers from Prison*, 397.

19. Bonhoeffer, *Letters and Papers from Prison*, 8.

follow the way of Jesus, we would open ourselves to the lives of other people, hear the real-life stories they have to share, pay special attention to the pain they experience, and listen for the voice of God. In this spirit, I listen for God in Black Sabbath.

2

𝔓rovidence of 𝔖orrow

The sound of rain creeps in. Thunder. A pregnant tor-rent. Then, a bell tolls—a signal of doom. *Bong . . . bong . . . bong.* This tension is held for almost a minute, before the band comes in, heavier than any rock music heard before it. *Boom . . . boom . . . boom.* E, octave E, B flat. On "Black Sabbath," guitarist Tony Iommi plays what in music theory is called a tritone, or "the devil's interval," and its effect in this song is undeniable. The band's goal was to create the horror movie of songs, and their execu-tion is perfect. The music quiets, but retains its deep chill, as Tony keeps repeating those three notes. "What is this that stands before me?" Ozzy sings, his voice trembling, "Figure in black, which points at me / Turn around quick, and start to run / Find out I'm the chosen one." Darkness has named its victim. It is closing in. And then we hear Ozzy's singular, horrifying shrill: *"Oh nooo!"* The word trails off into the deep, and the instruments return with full force. Darkness has swallowed up its victim.

No band in the history of music has captured dark-ness better than Black Sabbath did with this song. It is a perfect unity of form and content. Up to that point, it was the most sinister sound that rock music could muster. No song before it could have prepared listeners for its musical twilight. And it took an abysmal and global experience of evil to make this music possible—a decade of assassinations, senseless killing, social unrest, state-sanctioned violence, and war. The world became accustomed to seeing injustices, atrocities, and worst case scenarios, unfolding even in their very homes, on television. Young people who came of age marching for civil rights and protesting the war in Vietnam were subjected to demonization and brutalization by an unrelenting state apparatus. When Martin Luther King Jr. was assassinated, Nina Simone dolefully announced, "The King of Love is dead."[1] Many could no longer believe that the universe is "moral," or that its "arc . . . bends towards justice," as Dr. King had said.[2] No, many began to feel, this world is fucking evil.

The viewpoint in "Black Sabbath" is decidedly one-sided. It is a picture of utter loss and hopelessness. "Satan's sitting there, he's smiling." Evil is happy, having conquered all. Sabbath denies a happy ending, and even any hope. They end the song with a desperate cry. The three opening notes are a certain announcement of doom, and the band maintains that extremism to the end, leaving listeners with the taste of despair in their mouths. They give voice to the trauma and pessimism in the world at the end of the 1960s.

And yet, I cannot help but notice that the song is a prayer, as it repeats the cry: "Please God help me!" I think of Paul's similar cry in the book of Romans: "Who will save me

---

1. Nina Simone, "Why? (The King of Love Is Dead)," Westbury Music Fair, April 7, 1968.

2. Martin Luther King Jr., "Remaining Awake through a Great Revolution," speech given at National Cathedral, March 31, 1968.

from this body of death?" (7:4).[3] Both are addressed to God, calling on God to come to their aid, bewailing an experience of darkness that is total and all-consuming. They are prayers of *lament*, prayers which are unique to sufferers.

Lament

A lament is an embittered complaint to God born of devastation and disappointment. Where God is worshipped as one who is "merciful and gracious, slow to anger, and abounding in steadfast love and faithfulness" (Exodus 34:6), the prayer of lament contradicts this testimony by calling out God's silence and apparent indifference to human suffering.[4] Lament sacrifices piety in favor of blunt truth—that the sufferer is heartbroken, disillusioned, and mad as hell. The experience of pain is too strong to deny, and in a lament the poet commits to expressing that pain, even if it means approaching sacrilege and blasphemy. There will be no sweeping my pain under the rug. God will hear about it, directly and frankly, in my own words.

The books of Job, Jeremiah, Lamentations, and the Psalms in the Bible provide countless examples of lament. In stark contrast to the affirmations of Exodus 34:6, one psalmist asks if God's love has "ceased forever," or if God has "forgotten to be gracious" (Psalm 77:8–9). In their pain, the psalmist questioned the very heart and nature of God, and suggested that God was being unfaithful. The psalmist knew what they were doing. They knew they were calling into question the foundation of Israel's life and

3. All biblical quotations are from the New Revised Standard Version, unless otherwise notated.

4. On lament, see Ellington, *Risking Truth*, as well as Brueggemann, "Costly Loss of Lament," and Brueggemann, "Shape of Old Testament Theology."

identity. But that is how intense their pain was. That is how dire their straits had become.

The word the psalmists used for this experience was *sheol*, which in our English Bibles is often translated as "hell."[5] Hell is an important concept for Black Sabbath. They rely heavily on the dualism of heaven and hell. The album cover for "Sabbath Bloody Sabbath" infamously displays an illustration called "The Rape of Christ" by artist Drew Struzan.[6] In his Sabbath illustration, Struzan depicted demons descending upon Jesus, on a mattress covered in silk sheets. Hovering above them is a headboard, which is Satan himself, who stretches his arms across the bed, "666" carved into his rigid frame. On the back of the album, a contrasting scene is shown. A man lies peacefully unconscious, under a vibrantly colored blanket and resting his head on glowing pillows. He is surrounded by young people who are mourning his passing. The bed's headboard depicts a bird enveloping the earth. Standing behind the headboard is the shape of a large, muscular man, his head out of frame, leading us beyond the image. Father, Son, and Holy Spirit are all present for this heavenly occasion. The dominant colors of this tableau on the back of the album are cool and serene: blue, green, and silver. This array contrasts with the feverish colors on the front: chiefly, a neon, pinkish red. This dualism of heaven and hell runs throughout Sabbath's career—it is even the title of the first Black Sabbath-Dio album of 1980 (*Heaven and Hell*). Like a lot of biblical literature, Sabbath utilizes contrasts to offer, on the one hand, a vision of wholeness and goodness, and on the other, a vision of horror and misery.

5. Harris, "*Sheʾol*," 892.

6. Drew Struzan is also responsible for the original *Star Wars* posters.

Hell figures into lament when the sufferer can see no way out of her pain, when all seems utterly lost. "I am counted among those who go down to the Pit, I am like those who have no help. . . . I am shut in so that I cannot escape" (Psalm 88:4, 8). While most laments turn to praise in the Bible, others are not so reassuring. Sometimes the complaint is left unresolved, as the cry for God's help remains the only indication that change may be possible.

In chapter 3 of the book of Job, Job speaks of hoping for light but having none, of longing for death and regarding only the dead as happy. He spits out the Hebrew word *hoshek*—darkness—again and again, continually scratching for harsher ways of describing his despair—thick darkness, deep darkness, gloom, dread.[7] "I am not at ease, nor am I quiet," he says, "I have no rest; but trouble comes" (3:26). He makes no attempt at moderation or balance, shows no desire to account for diversity of experience. In this moment, there is only pain and utter outrage. How dare reality be like this! I will *not* calm down. I *will* make a scene. I will be *inconsolable*. "My wound is incurable" (34:6).

Sabbath practices this one-sided expression of pain in much of their music. A good example is the song "Solitude." It is like a psalm of lament in more ways than one, as it utilizes parallelism, a common tool for psalmists, which seeks poetry through repetition.

The song begins with the lyric: "My name, it means nothing, my fortune is less." Pain compels the sufferer to utterance, as he spirals into a negative hysteria. Yet this first absolute statement was not horrible enough—it failed to capture the intensity of the sufferer's pain. He had to say it again, but with new words. "My future is shrouded in dark wilderness / Sunshine is far away, clouds linger on." The sentiment is intensified through repetition in new form.

7. Alden, "*hoshek*," 331.

The sufferer does not relent. He beats the dead horse. Ozzy sings, my name means "nothing"; "everything" I had is gone; "nothing can please me"; and "all I do" is brood and cry. By continuing to rephrase in extremes, the sufferer clarifies his despair. To deliver these lines and mean them is to give voice to the deepest suffering. One must cry many times before one is able to write a song so full of tears. Ozzy sings with pathos and seriousness, Geezer plays a moody bass line, Iommi weaves in a haunting flute—a musical configuration that bottles sadness.

The alternative to lament is denial.[8] Believers who do not allow themselves to lament turn their life of faith into a life of escapism and repression. Indeed, many Christians live just this life, and struggle to sustain it. Many reject faith altogether after bearing the stress of perpetuating denial. One can only suppress one's pain for so long. Sabbath wrestles with this experience, in songs like "Wheels of Confusion" and "Sabbath Bloody Sabbath," which express the struggle of shedding illusions and confronting harsh reality. What they refuse to do is deny what they are feeling.

Pain must be felt. Sometimes life is just that horrible. And when we feel pain, nothing is less helpful than when we or others anxiously try to conjure up happy thoughts. Doing so only prolongs and intensifies despair, as what we experience contradicts the happiness we strive toward. To lament is to be honest. It is to speak truthfully about the pain we experience. As such, it can only be relentless. It can only be one-sided. A proper lamentation must be painful even to hear.

8. Brueggemann, "Costly Loss of Lament," 60.

Mental Anguish

In his volume on Black Sabbath's *Master of Reality* for the 33 1/3 book series, writer John Darnielle took an innovative approach to album commentary.[9] Instead of writing extended liner notes, which is the norm of the series, he wrote a fictional diary of a young mentally ill Black Sabbath fan who had been institutionalized. The first several entries are rather short and consist of defiant, all-caps curses, which the young man has angrily scratched into his diary. In further entries, however, he has adapted enough to his environment to begin to use the diary to write about his favorite album—*Master of Reality*. The only commentary and information we receive about the album comes through the voice of this troubled teen. Darnielle's book is remarkable for this ingenious framework. It is almost as if he, a musician and novelist, thought it too boring to write a straightforward work of nonfiction. Or maybe he thought such a book would not do the Sabbath album justice. Whatever the reason, his approach highlights an important aspect of Sabbath's art and life—specifically, that it appeals to young people who suffer mental illness.

> Finished with my woman 'cause she couldn't help me
>   with my mind
> People think I'm insane because I am frowning
>   all the time
> All day long I think of things, but nothing seems to
>   satisfy
> Think I'll lose my mind if I don't find something to
>   pacify

These lyrics open the title track "Paranoid" from Black Sabbath's second album. With them, the listener is hurled

9. Darnielle, *Master of Reality*.

into a difficult and heavy experience of mental anguish. For the sufferer, this experience disrupts relationships, creates social awkwardness, stirs agonizing restlessness, and even seems to bring him to the brink of insanity. Anyone who has had these experiences recognizes them immediately in Sabbath's lyrics, in part because of how blunt the expressions are. This first verse opens and closes with "my mind," and enclosed therein is a frenzy of extreme activity. "People think I'm insane because I am frowning all the time." Here is one of the greatest lines written about mental illness in rock music history. It captures the lonely experience of suffering which alienates one from others while simultaneously stigmatizing the sufferer.

I myself was an "emo kid," which is what we called those teens who dressed in black, tight clothes, who straightened their long hair, and were more often than not consumed by negative emotions. The very term "emo" referred to our "emotional" character. I know the feeling of being alienated and stigmatized for "frowning all the time." I once had a friend threaten to smack me every time he saw me with my head down (which apparently was often). When I listen to "Paranoid," it reminds me that I am not alone, that there are others who share my experience, who know my depression.

Depression is a peculiar pain. It is not like a physical pain which comes involuntarily when one is struck, nor is it like the pain one feels when one mourns the loss of someone or something. It is not necessarily occasioned by a specific occurrence. It is more an underlying, lasting, mortal anguish which often leads one to be obsessively preoccupied by fundamental questions of existence. The one who suffers depression is one-sidedly consumed by negative thoughts. Look at how many phrases in "Paranoid" suggest ultimacy: "finished with my woman"; "frowning all the time"; "all day long I think of things"; "nothing seems to satisfy"; and "think I'll lose my mind." These are all extreme phrases, and they occur one right after another, suggesting a frenzied mental state in which one is tormented by stark binaries: sanity vs. insanity, everlasting peace vs. everlasting turmoil, heaven vs. hell. This suffering seems to threaten everything. All is at stake, all life and goodness hang in the balance.

"Paranoid" describes an experience of incredible angst. The song is aptly titled. Its lyrics depict anxiety and depression, wherein the sufferer is in a state of utter mental peril. "Happiness I cannot feel and love to me is so unreal." The negative thoughts have taken over. Darkness has rubbed out all the lights. It is little wonder why critics derided Sabbath's albums as "downer music."[10] Mick Farren in *NME* magazine even said their music "probably causes brain damage."[11]

So that's it, then, right? Is there nothing left to do but go insane, kill yourself, or escape into drug use? To the uninitiated, this may seem to be what the song is saying, and many a metalhead have faced charges of inspiring hopelessness and promoting suicide. There was even a case of a nurse who killed herself while the *Paranoid* album was on her turntable, and an inquest was made to determine whether Black Sabbath bore some responsibility.[12] Ozzy Osbourne was later sued twice (both times, unsuccessfully) by different parents after their Ozzy-head sons committed suicide. But for someone who knows the experience that these lyrics detail, nothing is sillier than the idea that one could have suicidal ideation spontaneously injected into their minds through a song.

10. Wall, *Black Sabbath*, 100.
11. Wall, *Black Sabbath*, 126.
12. Iommi and Lammers, *Iron Man*, 83.

What is more, encountering our own experience of suffering in a song can actually be a significant source of healing. It is called *catharsis*, which, in therapy, "involves experiencing repressed emotional traumas within a safe environment."[13] In catharsis, one allows oneself to feel the unthinkable. One can, so to speak, *let loose* the emotions that drive internal anguish. Giving up the attempt to maintain balance, one is able to let the emotions take their course. We experience a measure of healing as we breathe through the experience, instead of trying to control or suppress it.

Cathartic poetry is extreme and relentless. It makes no attempt to resolve the emotional experience into some higher order. Since anxiety constitutes a breakdown of any such order, to onerously attempt to resist emotion in an effort to maintain order only serves to exacerbate anxiety.

I am not the first to recognize the real therapeutic potential of Sabbath's music. Philosopher Greg Littmann also made this connection, likening Sabbath's music to Aristotle's concept of catharsis. "In their bleakest songs," Littmann says, "we are invited to sympathize with people who are suffering."[14] I would add, however, that with Black Sabbath's music the experience is not just one of sympathy with one who is suffering, but actually inviting listeners to feel their own suffering through the suffering simulated in songs like "Solitude" and "Paranoid." Academic studies have been done highlighting these effects. Professor Jeffrey Arnett surveyed 175 males from ages fourteen to twenty and found that heavy metal music helped them purge negative emotions. Another study involving thirty-nine males from ages eighteen to thirty-four found that the music "relaxed listeners as effectively as sitting in silence." Professor

13. Longe, *GEP*, s.v. "Catharsis."
14. Littmann, "Art of Black Sabbath," 70.

Brett Barnett cited these studies to highlight the cathartic function of Sabbath's music.[15]

Black Sabbath gives listeners permission to feel their despair. Songs like "Paranoid" give you a few minutes to bear your pain, to hold it and perhaps even let it go. It is edifying to have such music, not only because it makes us aware that our suffering is a shared experience, and not only because it provides a safe moment to have that experience, but also because the music pushes us through the experience and beyond it. The music itself is uplifting. I mean, it doesn't take a dark-eyed goth to tell you this song fucking *rocks*!

"Paranoid" reached number 4 on the United Kingdom singles chart in 1970 and is today widely considered one of the greatest rock songs of all time. Ward's driving beat, Iommi's inspired guitar playing, and Ozzy's frantic vocals make for an infectious headbanger. Iommi plays eighth notes of a muted E power chord, then steps down to D, creating anticipation, before the drums and guitar clamor together on the three last syllables of each lyric ("with my mind" = *boomboomboom*). Iommi follows these three hits with a quick guitar stab, striking high D-G-B notes: "*Aack!*" The effect is thrilling, and wonderfully addictive to play on the guitar. Every element comes together perfectly and creates a raucous energy. There is nothing depressing about it. It overflows with life.

That is the magic of Black Sabbath. The lyrics are about doom, they tell stories of depression, anxiety, death, and despair, and yet the music transcends these themes altogether. It is at once thoroughly negative and yet the utmost positive music. As the drummer Bill Ward even said,

15. See Arnett, "Adolescents and Heavy Metal Music," 76–98; Arnett, *Metalheads*, 19, 82; and Sharman and Dingle, "Extreme Metal Music and Anger Processing," 1–11, cited in Barnett, "Black Sabbath's Pioneering Lyrical Rhetoric," 86.

he felt the music was "completely good and wholesome."[16] Through their cathartic engagement with the darker realms of human experience, Black Sabbath offers listeners a release from the intense pressures that so define the life of a troubled mind.

Sweet Re*leaf*

In an early interview, Black Sabbath was asked what they do to relax. "Smoke marijuana," Ozzy quickly responded, chuckling. A reporter responded, unblushingly, "You were joking when you said that," to which Ozzy said, "Yeah, right," laughing all the more. Then other members of the band chimed in, refusing to shy away from endorsing the drug. "It should be reviewed in a completely different manner, I think," the drummer Bill Ward remarked. "There's a lot *down* on it, but there isn't much *for* it."[17] This exchange reminds me of the 1984 mockumentary *This Is Spinal Tap*. It is not exactly an exceptionally articulate case for cannabis, but in a time when one could regularly encounter advertisements claiming that marijuana turns harmless people into psycho killers, Sabbath advocating the drug with aplomb is a nice counterpoint.[18]

And so Black Sabbath wrote a love song to cannabis. "Sweet Leaf," from the album *Master of Reality*, is a celebration of dope, a simple ode to the pleasant experience of getting high. But, looking closely, we can see the band is not just being playful (although "Sweet Leaf" is certainly a playful song, engaging the human love for playfulness). I contend that the song is also a note of appreciation from

16. Wall, *Black Sabbath*, 85.

17. ReelinInTheYears66, "Black Sabbath—Interview 1973."

18. See Alexandra, "Insane World."

a patient to his medication. Many today can attest to the therapeutic effects of cannabis for treating depression and anxiety, and for me that experience has opened up a new appreciation for this song.

"My life was empty, forever on a down / Until you took me, showed me around." The opening lines name the symptoms that weed treats for the band. Weed can offer a door to exit a spiral of negativity and enter an uplifted state of clarity and joy. We can take a breath, we can step away from our internal angst and enjoy ourselves a while. That is the promise of weed for Black Sabbath. This book itself owes something to the existence of weed, as Geezer Butler, the main lyricist, expressed: "Smoking dope was great for coming up with lyrics."[19]

This relationship with marijuana cannot be reduced to some adolescent affinity for amusement and laziness. It is the experience of someone who suffers greatly and has found a way to mellow out and regain a sense of equilibrium. "My life is free now, my life is clear"—certainly an overstatement, but it stands in happy contrast to "Paranoid," where the sufferer is never satisfied and on the brink of insanity. "Sweet leaf" balances out the extremes of anxiety, bringing sweet relief.

While the extent to which cannabis can be useful for treating anxiety and depression is debated, and the evidence for and against can be contradictory, it is clear at least that the drug has demonstrated positive effects against depression for many users, when used in a controlled manner. As both the negatives and the positives of cannabis have been increasingly understood, so it has been increasingly decriminalized and adopted by professionals across the globe for

19. Wall, *Black Sabbath*, 68.

various medical uses.[20] When Ozzy sang in 1971, "Soon the world will love you, sweet leaf," he wasn't wrong.

But drugs are not all fun and games for Black Sabbath. Other songs witness to the dangers of drug use, especially the way it can turn into an escape. Songs like "Hand of Doom," "Snowblind," and "Looking for Today" describe how escapism through drugs is a self-destructive pattern. The good time will pass, and it can ultimately kill you. "Price of life is high / Now you're gonna die." This theme occurs in just about every Sabbath album. Life is full of horrors, and so we turn to escapist habits to pump pleasure into our lives, but unhealthy habits inevitably take their toll on the body.

Sabbath often utilized apocalyptic language to drive home their point about the dangers of drug abuse. The apocalyptic dualisms of life and death, light and darkness, paradise and misery, point to high stakes. If we continue too far down certain roads, certain doom is in store for us.

There are many horror stories of the band's alcohol and drug intake, and their debaucherous activity—many of which are detailed in Ozzy's and Iommi's autobiographies. Each member of the band became infamous for depraved and often revolting public intoxication. They demonstrated in their lives the self-destructive drug abuse they warned against in their lyrics.

It could be said that Black Sabbath earned the disapproval of conservative society with their excessive drug use and alcoholism, that they were essentially a cautionary tale of what happens when one embraces the "rock 'n' roll lifestyle." But, looking back, we can heed the warnings

20. See EMCDDA, "Medical Use of Cannabis." In 2020, the United Nations reclassified cannabis from a Schedule IV drug to a Schedule I drug, meaning cannabis is now internationally designated as a much less dangerous drug. See Kwai, "U.N. Reclassifies Cannabis."

the artists themselves signaled for us. We do not have to choose between seeing truth in Sabbath's art and acknowledging the unsustainable reality the artists lived. Geezer in his lyrics told the truth about his own experience, from which future generations could learn.

An academic study of Sabbath's catalog found that 60 percent of the substance abuse references in Sabbath lyrics are "negative," by which they meant "primarily negative language, imagery, and subjects (e.g., despair, hopelessness, darkness, dread)."[21] While the lives of the band members often demonstrated unfruitful and undesirable patterns of behavior, Geezer's lyrics told the real story. They signaled the call which the band themselves failed to heed, but which is nonetheless prophetic—to choose life over death.

"Sweet Leaf" and "Hand of Doom" are two sides of the same coin. Drugs can be helpful tools for regeneration and sustaining equilibrium, for grounding us in reality and enabling us to find joy. But drugs can also be used excessively and to our own detriment. By offering these guideposts, Black Sabbath shows us a path forward—a, so to speak, *sober* assessment of drug use.

The wrongful use of drugs has been well-explored in theological circles; the rightful use, less so. To what extent is cannabis helpful in worship and meditation, for example? The evangelical Christians with whom I grew up would scoff at such a notion. Drug use is sinful in their minds, and so incompatible with spirituality or piety. And yet, if I am rendered incapable of praise or prayer by a tortured, depressed state of mind, what use is religion for me or am I for religion?

---

21. Conway and McGrain, "Understanding Substance Use." While the study itself is helpful, Conway and McGrain's interpretations of the data are less helpful. I do not agree that "drug use was rarely a subject of heavy songs"—a statement their own data disproves. (Apparently they never heard that Black Sabbath are the originators of "stoner metal.")

By the use of weed, I myself have been able to shrug off the negativity that often determines my "sober" state of mind, and open myself up to positive spirituality.

All too often, the Christian life is pitted against mental illness and mental health treatment. I have seen ministers suggest that a Christian should never experience depression, that depression is a sign of lack of faith. The consequence of this theology is, either I magically overcome my depression through "faith in God's provision," or I am forced to despair of my faith and leave the church to look for aid elsewhere. The church can learn from Black Sabbath. Space must be made for the lived experience and medical treatment of mental illness in the church.

Characteristic of Black Sabbath is their relentless commitment to raw, troubling reality, as well as their willingness to advocate what respectable society tries to suppress. Sabbath models lament as an essential feature of an honest life, advocates the destigmatization of mental illness, and accepts that medical supplements can be embraced as gifts from God for the treatment of mental distress. Their honesty about ways people cope with this sorrowful life—for better and for worse—is as helpful theologically as it is liberating personally.

3

Apocalyptic Imagination

*B*ooommmmm. An E power chord. The song "War Pigs" stomps in, at about 110 bpm, gently waltzing. The guitar sounds like a growl, and the bass is deep. The sound waves open up like the gaping mouth of Behemoth. Listening to it, I feel like the speakers are threatening to expand and swallow me whole.

BoomBooommmm. E to D. The band has taken us deeper now. We can sense it coming, like an inaugural address. Sirens start ringing. The alarm is sounding, the tension is building. I think, "Ohh no . . . please . . . God . . . help . . ."

BaNah! Suddenly, two quick guitar hits—D-E—and now we're at 180 bpm. Bill Ward's high hat is full of energy, and Ozzy, frenzy in his lungs, begins to sing:

> Generals gathered in their masses
>
> Just like witches at black masses
>
> Evil minds that plot destruction
>
> Sorcerers of death's construction

Here we have a sinister picture indeed, a tyranny of death and evil. And it describes what in 1970 was a present reality. The United States had been bombing Indochina relentlessly for years, American troops were burning homes and villages belonging to Vietnamese noncombatants, and were raping Vietnamese women. The US government had created a system of horror, taking hundreds of thousands of lives, displaying humanity at its worst. Seeking a "breaking point," when the destruction they caused would become so terrible and devastating that the North Vietnamese could no longer sustain resistance, US politicians and military commanders were hellbent on making as much damage as they possibly could.[1]

What was it that enabled these officials to disregard the destruction and devalue the tremendous loss of life they were causing? Black Sabbath calls it evil. The officials bombing the hell out of Indochina were "evil minds that plot destruction / sorcerers of death's construction." They cause only "death and hatred to mankind," as they create a "war machine" that dehumanizes others and imposes their capricious and destructive purposes on the world. "Politicians . . . started the war," but they leave the fighting "to the poor," indicating a caste system based not on right and the common good, but on corruption and violence. But, Sabbath promises, "Wait till their judgment day comes." Black Sabbath leaves no room for Blaise Pascal's sentiment, "To understand is to forgive," nor Gene Knudson's, "An enemy is one whose story we have not heard." The band harbors no sympathy for murderers, no interest in commiserating with those who destroy the earth, in hearing their side or extending empathy toward them. Relentless evil demands relentless judgment.

1. See Lawrence, *Vietnam War*, 91, 145.

> Day of judgment, God is calling
>
> On their knees, the war pigs crawling
>
> Begging mercy for their sins
>
> Satan laughing, spreads his wings
>
> Oh lord, yeah!

Sabbath declares the destroyers will meet a more ultimate destruction. Darkness will swallow up everything they have accumulated and built. They will become like the ashes of the bodies they burned. This overwhelming darkness will be God's judgment, and they will be helpless before it. Just as Jesus said many would plead to enter the kingdom of heaven and be met with the cold response, "I do not know where you come from. Depart from me, all you workers of evil!" (Luke 13:24), so Sabbath depicts the "war pigs" pleading for mercy and hearing only Satan's laughter in response.

Apocalypse and Retribution

The theology in "War Pigs" is pretty hardcore. It assumes that the ones waging war know that what they are doing is evil. They know it, and they are nonetheless doing it, plotting destruction, lying about it, and manipulating others to their sinister ends. God said to the prophet Jeremiah, "Shall I not punish them for these things? Shall I not avenge myself on such a nation as this?" (Jeremiah 5:29 NKJV). The abolitionist Frederick Douglass quoted this verse at the end of his first autobiography, indicting the American nation built on slavery.[2] Apocalyptic imagination maintains a commitment to a theology of retribution, which promises that God will have the last word and those who oppress people and destroy the earth will

2. Douglass, *Narrative*, 88.

suffer terrible consequences. Familiar with the apocalyptic literature in the Bible from his Catholic upbringing, Geezer Butler used its prophetic language to announce divine judgment on the US war machine. God will have vengeance on the war criminals, on a military-industrial complex that sacrifices human life on an altar of ideology.[3]

In an album review, music critic Lester Bangs called Black Sabbath "moralists"—a surprising descriptor given the band's reputation.[4] But it is not untrue. Geezer's lyrics are infused with a moral theology of retribution, akin to what we find in the book of Proverbs.

> Proverbs 11:23: "The expectation of the wicked is wrath." (NAS)

> Proverbs 22:8: "Whoever sows injustice will reap calamity."

> Proverbs 29:16: "When the wicked are in authority, sin flourishes, but the godly will live to see their downfall." (NLT)

Sabbath maintains this theology of retribution, insisting that evildoers will receive their just desserts.

Theologies of retribution are not as popular as they once were. Many find it difficult to get comfort from the idea that the wicked will get what they deserve in the end when the wicked are so often blessed with what they do not deserve here and now. As Chris Rock commented in his 2018 comedy special *Tambourine*,

> You know, some people never get theirs. Some people just *fail up*. People are like, "What goes

3. Doug Rossinow described the Vietnam War as "perhaps the most purely ideological war in U.S. History." Rossinow, *Politics of Authenticity*, 209.

4. Quoted in Wall, *Black Sabbath*, 98.

> around, comes around." No, it don't. Sometimes,
> it just keeps goin' around.

Indeed, the experience of watching a tyrant succeed in his evil endeavors is genuinely disheartening. It reveals that the worst *is* possible, that things can go horribly wrong, that goodness and decency are not necessary for success, and evil can get what it wants if given the opening.

And yet, this experience is also what makes a theology of retribution attractive. If good and evil are set for all eternity, and God ensures the victory of one over the other, then we can rest assured that, no matter what people do, no one will get away with evil in the end. It is perhaps because the idea of retribution is so attractive that it is so hard to believe—a too-good-to-be-truism. Gone are the days when it was commonplace to believe that evildoers will be punished in the end, that there is an undesirable place reserved especially for them, where Satan eagerly awaits the next batch of deplorables. Is this theology not a kind of wish-fulfillment, in which we outmaneuver reality and grant ourselves justice ahead of time?

Friedrich Nietzsche argued that the theology of retribution is "the cleverest revenge," because it transforms a temporal loss into an eternal win. Morality, he said, is a "revolt of the slaves," in which underdogs gain the upper hand by obligating their overlords toward charity. Accordingly, theology of retribution has less to do with promoting the good and more to do with demoting the powerful. It is the revenge of the weak against the strong.[5]

Nietzsche's description is not far off from Black Sabbath's theology of retribution. The band revels in God's judgment of the wicked. "On their knees, the war pigs crawling / Begging mercy for their sins / Satan laughing

5. Nietzsche, *Genealogy of Morals*, 19–20.

spreads his wings." This verse is striking for how unabash-
edly ruthless it is. Rarely does one encounter in modern
Christian thought this kind of unrelenting condemnation.
Generally, Christians are encouraged to, as Jesus said, "Love
your enemies, and pray for those who persecute you" (Matt
5:44). Conversely, Christians are usually discouraged from
reveling in animosity or gloating over the misfortune of
others. In accordance with these principles, worship songs
rarely feature such contempt for the wicked as we see in
"War Pigs." But perhaps that is precisely one of the limitations of the liturgies we encounter in church.

The Bible bears no such limitation. It is full of animosity toward those who abuse power and oppress the vulner-
able. As the rabbi Abraham Joshua Heschel said, the Bible
models "righteous indignation" as a positive manifestation
of anger. The prophets especially embodied "impatience
with evil,"[6] and nursed a belief in divine retribution:

> Jer 21:14: "I will punish you according to the
> fruit of your doings, says the Lord."

> Isa 3:11: "Woe to the guilty! How unfortunate
> they are, for what their hands have done shall be
> done to them."

The psalms, too, invoke this act-consequence theology.
Especially in the psalms of lament, the psalmist cries out
to God for justice, that the righteous will be exalted and oppressors will be cut down. Psalm 137, written by Israelites
in exile in Babylon, proclaims,

> O Daughter of Babylon,
>> doomed to destruction,
> Blessed is he who repays you
>> as you have done to us.

6. Heschel, *Prophets*, 363, emphasis original.

Blessed is he who seizes your infants,

and dashes them against the rocks. (vv. 8–9)

Damn. The Bible is *metal*. Metal is intense, extreme, heavy, bitter, harsh, vivid, and dramatic. The Bible is all of these things. It makes space for the full range of human experience, including those aspects of life that the church tends to leave out—*rage* toward the unjust, profound *grief* in the face of devastation, and *revulsion* toward oppressors. So while the "War Pigs" lyrics might not impress Christian ethicists, they are biblical in their contempt for oppression and in the gratification they feel in prophesying a grim fate for all who make life a living hell.

And why not? Nietzsche's argument against morality rests on the assumption that the "strong" do not deserve the attack that the "weak" level against them. The strong, he said, see goodness in themselves, while the weak see badness in their plight. The weak grow to resent the disparity and so deem the strong bad and themselves good.[7] But if the weak are "weak" precisely because they are the conquest of the "strong," then the origin of morality is not in the resentment of the undeserving, but in the harm done by those who abuse power.

One does not have to invent "the bad" if one is the victim of it. When one suffers evil, it is certain that it is evil. To return to Frederick Douglass, as a formerly enslaved person, he did not need anyone to tell him that slavery was evil, for he encountered it himself as horrifying, harmful, detrimental to his life and flourishing, and therefore absolutely unacceptable. In this experience, Douglass discovered morality, knowing intimately and spontaneously that it is evil to deny another person's humanity and enslave them, and it is good to honor the humanity of others and protect their

7. Nietzsche, *Genealogy of Morals*, 10–11.

freedom. Douglass acquired *moral authority*, the ability to draw a line in the sand and say no to one reality and yes to another. He did not need to enter a philosophy program to have his assertions about morality assessed by the most critical Western minds, who only pontificate about slavery, and who might encourage Douglass to concede nescience on the inner workings of the universe. No matter what anyone would say to him regarding morality, Douglass knew that slavery is evil and freedom is good.

Black Sabbath has no need to blush when Nietzsche criticizes retribution theology for its vengeful character. It might be severe, but it is just. Morality is not a clever revenge crafted by underachievers, it is the complaint of truth and justice. As Heschel wrote, "There are moments in history when anger alone can conquer evil."[8] If there will be no outrage when people use their power for evil, then there will be no resistance to evil and no abundant life. We not only *should* be able to protest the evil in the world and judge those who make way for it, it is paramount that we do so.

The Prophet's Burden

By now, in the tumultuous 2020s, it has become bitterly obvious that we cannot rely on people to be good. All too often, conscience fails to kick in at the eleventh hour to stop people from doing horrible things. Nor can we depend on institutions to protect us from injustice. If we are to have good in this world, we must fight for it. Goodness is not a given, it is a commitment, it is precious cargo we must protect the whole way down. Prophets with apocalyptic imagination understand this precarious situation. They warn us not to live our lives frivolously, or prance along like

8. Heschel, *Prophets*, 381.

innocent children who trust their parents to do what's best for them. We must pay attention and take responsibility or we will end up in a hell of our own making.

> Reflex in the sky
> Warn you you're gonna die
> Storm coming, you better hide
> From the atomic tide . . .

> Dying world of radiation
> Victims of man's frustration
> Burning globe of obscene fire
> Like electric funeral pyre

These lyrics, from Black Sabbath's song "Electric Funeral," paint a picture of a world destroyed by atomic bombs. The band members were born just a few years after the United States bombed Hiroshima and Nagasaki, and they were teenagers during the Cuban Missile Crisis, when the United States and the Soviet Union came frighteningly close to nuclear war. If any events should make clear to us the stakes involved in our collective choices for good or evil, it would be these. From them we learn that it is indeed humanly possible to obliterate millions of lives, destroy whole civilizations, and create immeasurable misery and suffering on the earth. Not only is it possible, but there are those in power who are actually invested in doing just that.

Today, it is not just nuclear war that threatens life on earth, it is the radical degeneration of the earth's environment due to human overreach. We are witnessing our world overwhelmed by the levels of carbon dioxide we are pumping into it. We can see natural habitats falling apart, ecosystems disintegrating, species approaching extinction, and whole arrays of wildlife struggling to survive. We can see that the right things are not happening, the course is not being corrected, restoration is not being expedited, and people in power are not looking out for the common good. And the climate is not taking this neglect in stride. It is not forgiving. It is unfolding exactly as the natural processes dictate. Acts do have consequences—and unfortunately the rain falls on the just and the unjust.

At my church in Brooklyn, we often sing, "All shall be well, and all shall be well, and all manner of thing shall be well." Black Sabbath is not so sure. They harbor a dread-filled sense that things will not turn out well. We may end up witnessing an epic global funeral. For prophets are under no obligation to provide reassurances. Audaciously, they inform us, the worst is about to happen if we let it. This may seem insufficiently hopeful, but prophecy concerns itself with the truth and not with human desire for solace and comfort. The prophet counters that it is precisely the preoccupation with self-comfort that enables so many to neglect the common good and abdicate responsibility. If the truth is bleak, it only makes the prophet's message more urgent.

Nonetheless, prophets take no joy in delivering their message. "The word of the Lord has become for me a reproach and derision all day long," Jeremiah complained; it is "a burning fire shut up in my bones; I am weary with holding it in" (20:8–9). The prophet's life is marked by suffering and not a little anxiety. It is agonizing to behold the status quo, to see the path on which we tread, and the stubbornness with which we stick to it, to know the consequences, and yet to be powerless to stop it. How painful it is to know the greatness and beauty that could be, and yet to see what is. Black Sabbath shares this pain, as in their song "Solitude," when they cry unceasingly as they envision a future "shrouded in dark wilderness." Their tears join the tears prophets have cried throughout centuries.

Jesus in the first century looked on Jerusalem "and wept over it," lamenting, "If you, even you, had only recognized on this day the things that make for peace!" (Luke 19:41–42). Prophets do not just warn, they beg: "O land, land, land! Hear the word of the Lord!" (Jeremiah 22:29). And when catastrophe is not avoided, the prophet is devastated:

> My joy is gone, grief is upon me,
>> my heart is sick. . . .
> For the hurt of my poor people I am hurt,
>> I mourn, and dismay has taken hold of me. . . .
> Oh that my head were a spring of water,
>> and my eyes a fountain of tears,
> so that I might weep day and night
>> for the slain of my poor people! (Jeremiah 8:18, 21; 9:1)

In this section of the book of Jeremiah, it is not clear where the words of God end and where Jeremiah's begin. Prophets feel the pain of God. They feel the pain of opportunities lost, of justice unrealized, of goodness and glory unseen. They feel the hurt of truth when lies take hold. The memory of justice stings in their hearts when murderers walk free, when the innocent are executed. Their bowels quake with grief.

This pain alienates the prophet. People generally prefer to avoid acknowledging consequences. We tend to have an acute allergy to bad news and calls to change our ways. We don't like negative vibes or people who kill the mood. Consequently, the prophet is not very popular, and is often punished or even killed for speaking truth to power. The prophet Micaiah was imprisoned for predicting disaster for a king's military expedition (1 Kings 22). "I hate him," the king said, "for he never prophesies anything favorable about me" (v. 8).

Jeremiah was beaten and imprisoned for accurately prophesying that the king of Babylon would lay siege to Jerusalem and make the Judeans his subjects (Jeremiah 37–38).
Jesus was crucified for prophesying the coming kingdom of
God under the Roman empire. Martin Luther King Jr. and
Malcolm X were assassinated for witnessing to the brutality
white Americans subjected black Americans to. "They hate
the one who reproves in the gate," said the prophet Amos,
"They abhor the one who speaks the truth" (5:10).

For the prophets in the Bible, God's judgment comes
in the form of the natural consequences which inevitably
follow unjust actions. Amos judged the powerful for op-
pressing the poor and neglecting those in need (8:4–6). He
said the day of the Lord would not be for them a day of
glory and heavenly joy, but darkness.

> Alas for you who desire the day of the Lord! . . .
> Is not the day of the Lord darkness, not light,
>   and gloom with no brightness in it? (5:18, 20)

Here, Amos sounds much like Black Sabbath in "War
Pigs" and "Electric Funeral." Doom awaits the evildoer.
Those who destroy the earth will be destroyed. This will
be divine justice.

It is not that prophets have some magic power to see
into the future; rather, they understand the consequences
of injustice. They are tuned in to the movements of history,
to the sowing and the reaping, to the chickens going out at
dawn and returning to roost at dusk. The prophet's words
are always coming true, in every age. Based on their knowledge of deeper things, they see what's coming, they see the
writing on the wall. With this insight, they issue a warning: sow justice, or reap catastrophe. "Turn back, turn back
from your evil ways and live," the prophet Ezekiel begged—
"for why will you die, O house of Israel?" (Ezekiel 33:11).

Today, countless people are choosing death by not doing their part to stop the spread of COVID-19. The pain we suffer witnessing this massive plunge into death is the pain the prophet bears. If only we chose life.

The Subversive Character of Apocalyptic Literature

While apocalyptic theology these days is commonly associated with conservative, end-times folks, Black Sabbath's lyrics turn the tables and deploy an apocalyptic theology against conservative Christian leaders. At the time "War Pigs" was written, Richard Nixon was using figures like Billy Graham to galvanize evangelical Christians, famously referring to them as the "moral majority." Meanwhile, he was carpet-bombing Cambodia. Criticizing this ideological war machine, Geezer took conservative theological material and turned it on its head, using it in Sabbath's songs to demonstrate the hypocrisy of Christians like Nixon. The supposed Satanist band thus became more Christian than the supposed Christians. With this cunning reversal, Sabbath's apocalyptic literature is strikingly similar to the cryptic book of Revelation—the Greek word for "revelation" being *apokalupsis*.

Biblical scholar Greg Carey describes the book of Revelation as a "counter-imperial script"—in other words, resistance literature.[9] Following a practice established by the apocalyptic book of Daniel in the Old Testament (Daniel 7:3), Revelation depicts the Roman empire as a beast from the sea (Revelation 13:1–5). And instead of naming Rome itself, the author often used "Babylon," recalling

9. Carey, "Book of Revelation," 157–76.

the prophetic books of the Hebrew Bible.[10] This coded language was strategic. The author put his prophecies in terms Roman authorities would not recognize. Writing in code was not just a creative choice, it was necessary for circulating the text incognito. Chapter 13 says the beast, Rome, received its power and authority from "the dragon" (v. 2), who is "the ancient serpent, who is called the Devil and Satan, the deceiver of the whole world" (Revelation 12:9). In other words, Rome is the enemy of God.

By the time Revelation was written, Christians in Asia Minor knew of the martyrdoms of John the baptizer, Jesus, the apostles Stephen, James, and Paul, and more recently a Christ-follower named Antipas (Revelation 3:13). Further, Christians under the Roman empire were regularly accused, brought to trial, and imprisoned—and conditions were only getting worse.[11] Given this context, it is clear the book of Revelation was written from the viewpoint of an oppressed people, and for the purpose of comforting and reassuring them that divine judgment and liberation were coming.[12]

Cloaked in mythological language, Revelation announced imminent doom for the Roman empire: "Alas, alas, the great city, Babylon, the mighty city! For in one hour your judgment has come" (18:9). The time will come

10. Traditionally, people refer to the author of Revelation as John, and the book itself is occasionally referred to as the "Apocalypse of John." However, the consensus is this name was added to the text. For this reason, I have chosen to refer to the author as anonymous.

11. In the early second century CE, not long after Revelation is thought to have been written, the Roman governor Pliny reported to the emperor Trajan that he regularly interrogated Christians concerning their allegiance to Christ, and executed them if they persisted in refusing to worship Roman gods, offer gifts to the emperor, and curse Christ. See Schüssler Fiorenza, *Book of Revelation*, 193.

12. Schüssler Fiorenza, *Book of Revelation*, v, 9.

for "destroying those who destroy the earth" (11:18). Merchants who "grew rich" off the imperial economy will "weep and mourn," for all the wealth of the empire will be "laid waste" (18:11, 17, 19). All "the rich and the powerful" will run and hide from "the wrath of the Lamb" (6:15–16). The forces of evil will be vanquished. Satan will be defeated, shackled, and imprisoned for a thousand years. During that time, the Christian martyrs who were executed by Rome will be resurrected and exalted to share in Christ's victory. Then Satan will be taken out of prison for the final act of God's victory over evil: he will be executed, just as Rome had executed Christians (20:1–10).[13] God will have vengeance and the earth will have justice.

Revelation describes God's victory in terms of military conquest, but God's means of conquering are radically different from the empire's. Victory is accomplished through "the Lamb" who was slain, referring to Jesus' martyrdom. Instead of achieving victory through violence, Jesus achieves victory through faithful witness and sacrifice—and not for the glory and prosperity of one nation, but for the good of the whole world.[14] Jesus' unrelenting commitment to justice and truth is the source of his power.

Conversely, imperial systems in the apocalyptic imagination are understood as driven and maintained by violence and a network of evil forces, which are supra-personal and yet effect destruction and misery on the earth. But with the victory of divine justice comes the abolition of all systems of oppression, even those which presently appear to be the most powerful. These systems are doomed because they exist through deception and injustice. But where empires fall, truth persists and cannot be destroyed.

13. For an illuminating commentary on Satan's imprisonment and execution in Rev 20, see Wood, "Alter-Imperial Interpretation."

14. See Bauckham, *Theology of the Book of Revelation*, ch. 4.

Revelation promises that those who remain committed to justice will be vindicated. The victims of the empire, and all those who are held in bondage, "from every tribe and language and people and nation" (5:9), will be made "priests" and "will reign on earth" in God's beloved community (5:10):

> God himself will be with them;
>> he will wipe every tear from their eyes.
>
> Death will be no more;
>> mourning and crying and pain will be no more.
>> (Rev 21:3–4)
>
> They will hunger no more, and thirst no more, . . .
> for the Lamb at the center of the throne will be their shepherd,
>> and he will guide them to springs of the water of life.
>> (7:16–17)

In celebration of the new world God inaugurates, the righteous will "sing a new song," which will be "like the sound of many waters and like the sound of loud thunder" (14:2). Loud, heavy, bombastic sounds will burst from heaven in victorious jubilee.

Black Sabbath's music is like these apocalyptic sounds. Bill Ward's clanging cymbals are like the crashing of waves, the pounding of his drums like the cracking of lightning. Ozzy's voice is a wolf's howl over the deep thunderous night of Iommi's guitar and Geezer's bass. "War Pigs" is apocalyptic music, it is the death knell of this world and the tolling of the new. This band, who once called themselves Earth, created the music of heaven.

Just like the book of Revelation turned Roman imperial imagery on its head with the image of the victory of the Lamb, Black Sabbath turned evangelical imagery on its head to criticize the US military-industrial complex. This system of oppression is doomed: "No more war pigs have the power / Hand of God has struck the hour." The power of God undermines the power of the war pigs, because the power of God is the power of truth. War pigs have no right-ful claim to their power and so cannot exist in perpetuity. Empires wield power to destroy and to spread lies, but Black Sabbath, echoing the book of Revelation, prophesied that only justice and truth can claim eternity.

4

From the Ruins of Birmingham

One of the defining traits of Black Sabbath as a group is their working class perspective. They were a band of guys from the British underclass, who actually experienced the dread and deprivation in their lyrics. Their working-class perspective occasioned in their music unrelenting antagonism toward the imperial status quo. They describe our world as intentionally designed for oppression, for the prosperity of some and the misery of most. Black Sabbath not only bemoan this order, they call for its destruction, and for radical systemic change. Black Sabbath's commitment to revolution is central to their theology.

Killing Yourself to Live

In his autobiography, Ozzy described what it was like to grow up working-class in Birmingham, UK. He recalled seeing his mother weeping when she could not afford to pay the bills.[1] When he got a job at a car horn factory as a teenager, he had to shout at the top of his longs in order for one of his coworkers to hear him because the coworker had suffered significant hearing loss from working in the factory for so long.[2] Ozzy was horrified by the extent to which this man had sacrificed his body to the factory. Ozzy called factory life a "trap," and he was desperate to get out of it.[3] This trap is poignantly captured by Sabbath's lyric, "You're only killing yourself to live." Under the guise of providing for themselves and being responsible, people sacrifice their own well-being and freedom.

"Making a living." That's what life's all about. "Getting by." These are things we say about our lives, about how we occupy *most* of our time. We get jobs we do not want and then we justify remaining in them because we have "got to make a living." People will tolerate all manner of abuse in the name of making a living. Ozzy, Iommi, Geezer, and Bill all knew what it meant to be killing yourself to make a living. Coming out of prison, Ozzy and Iommi took the bottom of the barrel of factory jobs, and felt sacrificed to the machines. Iommi's fingertips, which had already brought him some level of fame with a guitar at the age of seventeen, were sacrificed to factory machines. The modifications he was forced to make to his guitar so he could play without hurting his fingers determined what would become his classic guitar sound.

In his article "Factory Music: How the Industrial Geography and Working-Class Environment of Post-War Birmingham Fostered the Birth of Heavy Metal," Leigh Michael Harrison paints the picture of the starkly industrial environment of Birmingham in the 1950s and '60s:

1. Wall, *Black Sabbath*, 7.

2. Osbourne, *I Am Ozzy*, 30.

3. Osbourne, *I Am Ozzy*, 27.

> Almost two hundred years of continued industrial expansion meant that residential areas and schools were surrounded by factories, continually subjecting the city's children to the sounds of heavy industry.[4]

Everyday life was engulfed by industry sounds, as schools were next to factories, trains crisscrossed the city, and industrial plants could be seen almost anywhere. A 1946 Birmingham Public Health Department Housing Survey found that "noise and smoke from the factories hindered light and air from reaching the houses they surrounded."[5] Also present in every borough of the area were bombed-out buildings, remnants of World War II. Having been a key city in the production of arms, Birmingham was completely transformed by the war's destruction. All four members of Black Sabbath were shaped in some way by the poverty, industrial setting, and postwar depression that defined life in Birmingham in the mid-twentieth century.

Bassist and lyricist Geezer Butler inhabited a special intersection of this existence. He comes from an Irish background, his parents having been Dubliners before they moved to Birmingham. The Irish in the United Kingdom have a long history with discrimination and oppression, as in 1869 Karl Marx noted, "The English worker hates the Irish as a competitor who lowers his standard of life," even comparing how the Irish were treated to how white Americans enslaved and segregated black Americans.[6] In 1846, Frederick Douglass as a free man spent six weeks in Dublin, and was shocked by the poverty he witnessed there, writing in a letter, "Poor creatures! They

4. Harrison, "Factory Music," 145.
5. Harrison, "Factory Music," 147.
6. Karl Marx, quoted in Robinson, *Black Marxism*, 329n72.

are left without help, to find their way through a frowning world."[7] Traces of this history lie deep in Butler's lyrics.

The Industrial Revolution, which still formed the backdrop of life in factory-laden Birmingham in the 1950s when the Sabbath members came of age, left countless Irish and English workers in abject poverty, creating an environment of radicalization and doom. E. P. Johnson wrote in his 1963 book *The Making of the English Working Class* that industrialization had inaugurated an age "when men's psychic world was filled with violent images from hell-fire and Revelation, and their world was filled with poverty and oppression."[8] Echoing this history, Black Sabbath's music is an outburst of working-class English and Irish kids finding their way through a frowning world.

Each original member of Black Sabbath expressed that music was the path they followed to avoid working in a factory or going to prison. In their autobiographies, Ozzy and Iommi detailed their rough early lives and the physical tolls factory work took on them. In interviews, Geezer described a hometown full of bombed-out buildings and run-down homes, and Bill Ward said he would lie in bed at night and hear machinery pounding away, heavy sounds which came to influence his drumming.

Another defining aspect of this working-class Birmingham existence was the prison. Two of the band's four members—Ozzy and Iommi—experienced prison sentences at young ages, which undoubtedly shaped their character and their creativity. Ozzy in his autobiography recalled a story from his last days in prison when he encountered a friend he met while working at a slaughterhouse named Tommy. He asked Tommy how long he was in for, and Tommy said four years. All he had done was

7. Quoted in Blight, *Frederick Douglass*, 152.
8. Quoted in Moore, "Unmaking," 143.

steal cigarettes and candy bars. When Ozzy expressed disbelief at a four-year sentence for such petty thievery, Tommy explained, "Third offense. Judge said I hadn't learned my lesson."[9] Having committed his third offense, he had become, in the eyes of the state, a delinquent.

Michel Foucault outlined the category of the "delinquent" in his 1975 book *Discipline and Punish*. The European ideology justifying the rise of prisons, he wrote, involved a "dangerous individual," who "belongs to a typology that is both natural and deviant." The delinquent is contrasted with "the norm" as an individual and is found wanting. He is recognized as a naturally perverse "malefactor," a criminal subspecies of human.[10]

Delinquents are not given a punishment to fit their crime, they are sentenced to isolation and bondage to "learn their lesson." In monasteries, devout monks spent extensive amounts of time in isolation reflecting on how to ascend to holiness. With this example in mind, the logic of the prison assumed that if criminals were given the time to reflect on their actions in this way, they could change and better themselves.

The astounding fact about the continued use of the prison system, however, is that it has consistently proven unsuccessful in this rehabilitative purpose. As Foucault observed, the prison system has long been recognized "as the great failure of penal justice."[11] For all its funding and popular acceptance, incarceration has never brought down crime rates. Instead, recidivism rates are consistently high.

9. Osbourne, *I Am Ozzy*, 40–41.

10. Foucault, *Discipline and Punish*, 251–53.

11. Foucault, *Discipline and Punish*, 274. Michelle Alexander, writing almost two decades later in the American context, echoed this understanding, saying, "As a crime reduction strategy, mass incarceration is an abysmal failure." Alexander, *New Jim Crow*, 237.

More often than not, instead of "learning their lesson," offenders returning to society are put under surveillance, disqualified for most jobs, and consequently just a matter of time away from repeating criminal behavior.[12] Far from reducing crime, the prison system dooms people to a life of crime and punishment.

But a failure in one sense is a success in another. The state has failed with the prison system to improve society, but has succeeded, Foucault says, in "producing delinquency," which functions as "controlled illegality."[13] The judge did not send Ozzy's friend Tommy to prison to learn his lesson, but in order to take control of Tommy's life, to fix him into a system of domination. Now the state would always be able to keep an eye on this delinquent, monitor his behavior, and determine his future. No longer would he evade their grasp.

The prison system is not about solving the problem of criminal activity, but keeping a handle on the underclass the state has created. As one American defense lawyer remarked to journalist Matt Taibbi, "Low-class people do low-class things."[14] The point of prison is not to solve the problem of crime, but to keep "low-class people" under control. The ruling class depends on the immobility of the low-class. For some, they have constructed a school-to-factory pipeline. For the "abnormals," they have a reserve school-to-prison pipeline, and those who fall into it end up in a prison-crime cycle.

Ozzy, Iommi, and their friends were members of this "low-class" in the United Kingdom. They had experienced society swallowing them up and shitting them out. Having become the low-class material society did not want, they

12. Foucault, *Discipline and Punish*, 265–67.

13. Foucault, *Discipline and Punish*, 276–78.

14. Taibbi, *Divide*, 114.

gained a new perspective on the order of things around them.

> Just take a look around you, what do you see?
> Pain, suffering, and misery
> It's not the way the world was planned
> It's a pity you don't understand

Refusing to capitulate to a world hostile to them, Black Sabbath found a way out through music.[15] Faced with the options, "factory or prison," they declined to deem one preferable to the other. The factory is the prison for workers, the prison is the factory for the unemployed. These young Brits could not reconcile themselves with this arrangement of society. They set out to blaze their own path, insisting music is worthwhile on its own, and that the world should make an opening for people to make a living through art, through a chosen profession which involves not the denial but the affirmation of life. In their music, Sabbath witnessed to this alternative vision of society, and indicted the system of domination evident in their experience.

Wicked World

"The world today is such a wicked place," opens the song "Wicked World" on Sabbath's first album. Geezer wrote these lyrics having been familiar with the Christian interpretation of the world as enmeshed in sinfulness. For many manifestations of Christianity, "the world" is evil, and fleeing from the world is the Christian's only hope. Wickedness is made up of human activities which pour from desire—drinking

---

15. As Ozzy said in his autobiography, "Thanks to Beatlemania, it seemed all right that I didn't want to work in a factory." Osbourne, *I Am Ozzy*, 32.

alcohol, having sex, gambling, etc. Anything can be sinful if it stimulates the senses enough.

The development of Christian anxiety about witchcraft had much to do with this distrust of sensuality. The historian Lyndal Roper says witches in sixteenth- to seventeenth-century Germany were thought to have "abandoned themselves to sensual enjoyment, flying, drinking, eating, dancing and having sex." Consistently, she observed, fear of witches was connected to "a fundamental fear of libidinal energies," especially fear of women's sexuality and power. This fear manifested itself in fantasies of witch gatherings like the "witches' sabbath" (also known as "black sabbath"), where witches danced together, had sex with the devil, and even lined up to kiss his anus.[16] Today, we can recognize the sexually repressed character of these fantasies. It was, Roper says, "as if too much pleasure might destroy society itself."[17]

This assumption can be found in conservative Christian communities to this day. Growing up, my family and our church community were libido-phobic and obsessed with sexual "purity." When one of my family members casually equated the word "virgin" with "pure," I asked where exactly this equivalency came from, and while they insisted it was a natural pairing, they could not articulate how or why. But it was not just sexuality which was categorically suspect, our Christian community was generally suspicious of all entertainment. My dad once shrewdly explained to me that entertainment is meant to *retain* you from *entering* the kingdom of God. When I was thirteen, I wore a

16. Roper, *Witch Craze*, 113. The popular image of the witch flying on a broomstick, Roper says, also stems from this fear of women's sexuality. Riding in the air with their hair flowing in the wind "on a phallic rod, stick or fork, was a fantasy of sexual abandon." Roper, *Witch Craze*, 108.

17. Roper, *Witch Craze*, 123.

Beatles shirt to church and was genuinely surprised by how scandalized and judgmental people were. The Beatles are "secular," meaning "of the world."

Christians of the conservative variety seek to live separate from "the world." They condemn the world to hell and live only for the hope of heaven. They suppose that they are somehow not also a part of this world, not also shaped in countless ways by the events of world history. But whether they acknowledge it or not, their isolation from the world is only afforded them by a long-standing maintenance of secular power in the world. And their self-understanding relies on the *other* cultures of the world to serve as foils for their own poverty of culture. Their religion is not merely a commitment to going to heaven with Jesus when they die, it is just as much a transvaluation of that phantasmic entity they call "the world." What "the world" calls good, Christians are inclined to call bad, and if "the world" calls what they do and say bad, then it can only mean they are sharing in the persecution and suffering which Christ endured. Did not Jesus say, "Blessed are those who are hated . . ."?

The consequence of this construal of religion is that life is not taken seriously in its reality. Proximity to reality is proximity to wickedness, because they regard our world as essentially and hopelessly wicked. Why else would Jesus come to rescue us from it? And anyone who takes this world seriously, and finds in it the source of their joy and concern, is a heathen. To follow Jesus means to reject the wicked world and spurn the pleasures of life which exist outside the church.

Black Sabbath maintains an altogether different sense of the world's wickedness. For Sabbath, wickedness is injustice, and this wicked world is a world which has been violently structured into a caste system. As they describe in the song, the wealthy in high places eat, drink, and are

57

merry, they decide national priorities and get rich off industry, while the poor suffer miserable working conditions and lose loved ones to war. Both private and public sectors are implicated in this superstructure. There is no division between the family or congregation and "the world." Religion is secular, the world is religious. Family is political, politics is intimate. The way a society is organized has real-life implications for all its inhabitants, and the choices individuals make reverberate throughout the world. Injustice is not some ontological given inscribed as law into this inherently "wicked world." Injustice exists on purpose, and must be resisted with purpose. In their secular interpretation of the gospel, Sabbath comes closer to Jesus' actual message: resist this unjust world by loving your neighbors.

Also Christlike is Sabbath's focus on those who suffer—the poor, the imprisoned, and the oppressed (Luke 4:18–19). Ozzy sings about a single mother whose husband died in battle; her children are left alone, she works long hours to provide for them. This intimate experience of suffering is the result of global affairs, reflecting the way secular-political activity has personal-familial consequences. Sabbath points to "the least of these" rather than remain silent and ignore injustice.

"Wicked World" is a blues song. In the beginning, Black Sabbath was a blues band—the "Polka Tulk Blues Band," to be precise.[18] Commenting on the nature of the blues, liberation theologian James Cone wrote that "blues people believe that it is only through the acceptance of the real as disclosed in concrete human affairs that a community can attain authentic existence."[19] The blues wrestles with reality, and seeks to describe reality honestly. Blues

18. Heavy metal is often called "white-boy blues." Weinstein, *Heavy Metal*, 66.

19. Cone, *Spirituals and the Blues*, 113.

writers practice a demythologization that prefers honesty to niceness. As the *Norton Anthology of African American Literature* describes, the blues is "decidedly secular," it promises "no heavenly grace or home," but rather witnesses to "earthly trials and troubles."[20] It does not take you away from the world, or reject the world in favor of an illusion of isolation and a fantasy of paradise, but instead grabs reality by its horns, interrogates its depths, and finds an opening for transcendence.

When Black Sabbath picked up the blues, they found a way to tell the truth about the misery in their environment, and to transcend that misery through music. Ozzy recalls of his youth,

> In those days, the working person's mentality went like this: you got what little education you could, you found an apprenticeship, they gave you a shit job. And then you did that same shit job for the rest of your life.[21]

Consciously, Ozzy used his experience to testify to the reality of systems of domination, refusing to be lulled away by fantasies. He expressed this commitment as a defining feature of Sabbath's existence. The band was explicitly making music to highlight realities that go neglected, that many prefer to pretend do not exist. The blues as a musical genre was especially fit for this exercise.

"Wicked World" does not buy into the veneer of legitimacy that apologists for the status quo claim for it. Sabbath's song listens instead to those who suffer, those who are grieving and striving and dying. Having established this starting point, Sabbath takes a step further, condemning and opposing the illegitimate order that made such

20. "Blues," 48.
21. Osbourne, *I Am Ozzy*, 27.

suffering reality. Defying their struggle in Birmingham, the band created music that sounded like bursting through the factory walls.

Children of the Grave

Oppression is unsustainable. Eventually, something must erupt. The world must change. The oppressed must have the world changed. The need for this change, as the liberationist Frantz Fanon wrote, "exists in a raw, repressed, and reckless state in the lives and consciousness of colonized men and women."[22] The oppressed cannot abide oppression forever. They must have *revolution*. Black Sabbath witnesses to revolution in the song "Children of the Grave." Kept down by a world that hates them, the oppressed cry out and long for a better world. Like a volcano, they must erupt and pour out their consuming fire. "The children start to march."

Who are the "children of the grave"? In 1971, when *Master of Reality* was released, there were many suitors. In the United States, black Americans marched for their freedom, and their most prominent leaders had been assassinated. By 1971, Medgar Evers, Malcolm X, Martin Luther King Jr., and Fred Hampton were dead. The Civil Rights movement suffered a terrible blow with the death of King in 1968, and the Black Panther Party disintegrated following Hampton's assassination in 1969. By 1971, it seemed to many like the fight for black liberation itself was dead, their leaders "children of the grave."

Another suitor for Sabbath's moniker were the Vietnamese fighting for freedom in Southeast Asia. President Lyndon Johnson and Secretary of Defense Robert McNamara failed to understand that their opponents were

22. Fanon, *Wretched of the Earth*, 1.

FROM THE RUINS OF BIRMINGHAM

fighting for independence, for freedom from colonization. The colonized fight "until they've won," as Sabbath's song says. The Vietnamese were never going to give up and let an American imperialist arm come in and replace the French one. Hundreds of thousands of Vietnamese soldiers died fighting for independence from imperialism. And many Americans recognized their own commitment to independence in the North Vietnamese. Many of those protesting the war in Vietnam War took a pro-Viet Cong stance. As the boxer Muhammad Ali famously said, "I am not going 10,000 miles to help murder, kill, and burn other people simply to help continue the domination of white slavemasters over dark people the world over."[23] Similarly, Civil Rights lawyer Thomas N. Todd said many African American troops in Vietnam would "rather switch than fight."[24] The implication is that both African Americans and the North Vietnamese were fighting the same imperial power to accomplish liberation.

Closer to Black Sabbath's own cultural makeup, "children of the grave" also referred naturally to the general rebellion of British and American youth, which formed the basis of heavy metal culture. Deena Weinstein typified heavy metal culture as a community of "proud pariahs" and "symbolic rebels" who "invert the values of respectable society." Metalheads emphasize "the chaos which society seeks to keep at bay."[25] A decisive question, however, is to what end this rebellion is committed.

23. Quoted in Canwell and Sutherland, *African Americans in the Vietnam War*, 37–38.

24. Katz, *Capturing Sound*, 160. This quote was made famous by the hip-hop group Public Enemy, as it can be heard in the opening sample on their song, "Fight the Power."

25. Weinstein, *Heavy Metal*, 249.

Central to the counterculture of the late '60s and early
'70s was the question of authenticity. White, conservative,
bourgeois culture came with norms that dictated how
people should act and behave—how they dress, how they
talk, how they express themselves. For white youth, rock
and roll rebellion came out of a search for authentic self-
expression—that is, expression which coheres with inner
feeling over against outside expectations. Patriarchal society, from the outset, is indifferent and even antagonistic
toward feeling, and demands that individuals be alienated
from their own sense of self. Do not be who you are, be
who you *should* be—i.e., who the white father wants you
to be. Do not go out and pursue your own interests, stay
near the plantation, get married, join the family business.
The white youth of the late '60s / early '70s categorically
rejected these dictates of their white fathers. This rejection
of patriarchal standards in favor of authenticity constituted
the white youth's cultural rebellion.

But does rebellion mean revolution? Does cultural
rebellion necessitate an overhaul of the conditions that created the demand for self-alienation in the first place? In the
first half of the 1960s, the social upheaval among black and
white people in the United States was geared toward the
transformation of socioeconomic conditions. During the
civil rights movement, the white youth were finding personal liberation through the struggle for black liberation, and
an awakening among white people led to the formation of
the "new left," a movement of revolutionary intellectuals and
activists. But reactionary forces in the latter half of the 1960s
transformed this landscape. Assassinations, police brutality
against protesters, FBI sabotage efforts, and the Vietnam
War formed, to use a Black Sabbath phrase, a "providence
of sorrow" that severely wounded liberationist efforts, and
altered the character of the new left. Increasingly, the new

left, as Doug Rossinow tells it in his book *The Politics of Authenticity*, "grounded their political radicalism in their conviction of their own authenticity."[26]

This withdrawal into self had already been precipitated by the beats and other "symbolic rebels" of the 1950s. Albert Camus's *The Rebel* from 1951 influenced a generation of white intellectuals who considered revolutionary efforts futile, but judged worthwhile the pursuit of authentic self-expression and resistance to conformity—"the sublimation of the individual," in Camus's words.[27] The result was a leftist white culture that adopted the spirit of black radicalism without committing themselves to the work of transforming society. In 1957, Norman Mailer wrote his essay "The White Negro," advocating "hipsterism," which searched for authentic expression through imitation of black counterculture. Also in 1957, Jack Kerouac, in *On the Road*, described feeling disillusioned by being a white man and wishing he were black. Black people, as Amiri Baraka wrote, cannot help but be countercultural, because white society rejected and alienated them from the outset. In an attempt to become countercultural, white people followed black culture, adopting black styles in thinking, dress, speech, and music, believing that by transcending their whiteness they could become authentic human beings. Their aim was not justice and revolution per se, but rather nonconformity and self-actualization.

The 1960s would see a different generation of white people, one more devoted to the abolition of oppression and the hope of a beloved community. But by the end of the decade, when governmental authorities made clear their intention to violently resist social change, despair and cynicism

26. Rossinow, *Politics of Authenticity*, 206.

27. Camus, *Rebel*, 15. For his conception of rebellion versus revolution, see 250–52.

threatened to engulf the white counterculture. As journalist Andrew Kopkind wrote in 1967, "To be white and a radical in America . . . is to see horror and feel impotence."[28] To compensate this feeling of impotence, white radicals settled for rebellion. The result was a mere cultural revolution which, as Rossinow wrote, "stabilized the existing society by promoting a kind of social flexibility."[29] White cultural revolution paved the way for new acceptable forms of self-expression, but not for black liberation. Authenticity became another white privilege.

Heavy metal culture is part of this story. There is no doubt that heavy metal challenges authority, rejects the status quo, and defies white standards of respectability, but this symbolic rebellion is not always connected to a social consciousness that demands systemic change. Heavy metal values include ecstasy, catharsis, nonconformity, release of aggression, but not always political engagement.[30] Heavy metal is also defined by severe disillusionment, and is often shot through with cynicism and even misanthropy. Black Sabbath exhibits this tendency toward nihilism, as in "Wheels of Confusion":

> I found that life is just a game
> But there's never been a winner
> Try your hardest, you'll still be a loser
> The world will still be turning when you're gone

These declarations of meaninglessness, hopelessness, and nothingness threaten to blot out any opening for change. Consequently, the rebellion of nihilism encourages individuals to reject society in favor of themselves, as Ozzy

28. Kopkind, "They'd Rather Be Left," quoted in Rossinow, *Politics of Authenticity*, 187.

29. Rossinow, *Politics of Authenticity*, 293.

30. Weinstein, *Heavy Metal*, 272.

sings in "Under the Sun": "I just believe in myself 'cause no one else is true."

As we saw in our discussion of lament in Black Sabbath, their expression of nihilism comes out of experiences of deprivation, destruction, and disappointment. These feelings must be expressed, and Black Sabbath articulates them through heavy, ominous music, and extreme, foreboding lyrics. But cynicism is not where Black Sabbath's theology ends. Sabbath's nihilism is a moment in a larger movement from despair to transcendence.

"Children of the Grave" is Sabbath's anthem of revolution. In 1971, at a fragile point in the international struggle for revolution, Black Sabbath did not encourage resignation and withdrawal into self, but rather called for reinforced commitment: "Show the world that love is still alive you must be brave / Or you children of today are children of the grave." Here again, Sabbath is resisting escapism. We cannot abdicate responsibility and live only for our precious uniqueness.[31] We must resist and fight for a better world. Sabbath offered this message in a year when it seemed like all hope was lost, when freedom movements were beginning to degenerate, following crushing blows from the imperial establishment.

It is true that Sabbath's music is an invitation to reject society's definitions and standards in favor of one's own. Sabbath encourages defiance and the release of aggression. Their music is bleak and full of dread. But the music is also, consistently and without reservation, a call to refuse to accept things as they are, and to imagine and create other ways of being, based on love and justice rather than hate and violence. In Sabbath's music, the status quo has

31. In his last novel, James Baldwin wrote, "Not everything is lost. Responsibility cannot be lost, it can only be abdicated." Quoted in Glaude, *Begin Again*, xxix.

already been destroyed. Black Sabbath's theology refuses to accept the justifications for this world, and instead pronounces it fundamentally broken, an order of evil. But the "wicked world" is not to be escaped; rather, it is in need of destruction and reparation. Revolution, Sabbath tells us, is not a task we can evade. We cannot be rebels only. We must change this world.

5

𝕭lack 𝕾abbath and 𝕭lack 𝕳istory

B lack Sabbath was inducted into the Rock & Roll Hall of Fame in 2006, thirty-six years after the release of their first album. Sister Rosetta Tharpe, "the Godmother of Rock & Roll," was not inducted into the Rock & Roll Hall of Fame until 2018—eighty years after her first recordings were released.

Black Sabbath's original band name was the Polka Tulk Blues Band, and they performed songs that were written by Willie Dixon, John Lee Hooker, and Howlin' Wolf.[1] The band took musical forms that were invented by African American musicians and made them their own. Notwithstanding Sabbath's uniqueness, their music is an offshoot of black American blues. What's more, Black Sabbath's success was made possible by Beatlemania and the so-called British invasion of music into the United States.[2] Sabbath became

1. Wall, *Black Sabbath*, 30.

2. As Beatles tour promoter Arthur Howes remarked, "The biggest thing The Beatles did was to open up the American market to all British artists. . . . The Beatles made an enormous amount of money

a hot commodity because other British blues bands already were hot commodities, and those bands owed their success to African American musicians.[3] Black Sabbath thus benefited from the British colonization of blues music. And having made blues forms their own, each member of the band went on to make millions of dollars.

In this chapter, I will explore Black Sabbath's connection to black history, highlighting the blues in Sabbath's music, and asking what it means that white British working-class musicians in the United Kingdom became far more successful than the black American musicians who wrote the standards on which all British rock bands depended. Following this analysis, I will take up the ethical issues with white people adopting black musical forms, and what it says about Sabbath's music and the artists themselves.

Black Sabbath and the Blues

It goes without saying that Black Sabbath's music would not have been possible without the innovations of black musicians in the Unites States. Blues and rhythm 'n' blues came out of particular black American lives, lives shaped by slavery and segregation.[4] All too often it is forgotten

for this country." Quoted in Marwick, *Sixties*, 458. Here was Ben E. King's reception of this development: "All the signs were there that the music that was being created right here at home was gonna be tremendously big. And then all of a sudden these kids came along and stopped all that. It was a hard pill to swallow." Quoted in Werner, *Change Is Gonna Come*, 86–87.

3. Amiri Baraka called it "the harnessing of Black energy for dollars by white folks." Quoted in Ward, *Just My Soul Responding*, 110. Similarly, music historian Maureen Mahon noticed that with white rock 'n' roll bands, "black resources provide[d] white wealth." See Mahon, *Right to Rock*, 158.

4. See Oakley, *Devil's Music*, and Baraka, *Blues People*.

that every rock album owes something to the creativity of African American musicians like Bessie Smith, Robert Johnson, Rosetta Tharpe, and Little Richard. Our understanding of Black Sabbath's music will be enriched by reflecting on this history.

Rock musical templates were originally laid down by black gospel, blues, and jazz innovators who had to learn how to survive in a country built for white people. As James Cone wrote, gospel music and the blues both invite the listener "to move close to the very sources of Black existence, and to experience the Black community's power to endure and the will to survive."[5] Rock music's ability to powerfully express emotion, and get people moving while doing it, is no accident. It came out of a human need to overcome circumstances, to express suffering and create joy. Rock embodies the energy and drive of gospel music, as well as what Cone called the "secular spiritual" quality of the blues, as the music insists on being grounded in life and open to the present moment.[6]

Blues lovers will often say that blues cannot be imitated, but must be *felt*. As Craig Werner wrote, "the most fundamental blues question" is, as Bob Dylan sings in "Like a Rolling Stone"—"How does it feel?" The blues, Werner continues, is "about how it feels to be existentially adrift, a broken piece of a fallen world."[7] Black Sabbath is an example of a band that did not seek to imitate the blues, but sought to follow after that blues spirit and feel their way toward musical creativity. The Beatles and the Beach Boys copied guitar parts by Chuck Berry. Robert Plant and Mick Jagger imitated blues singers. But Black Sabbath used blues and jazz forms as jumping-off points for their own

5. Cone, *Spirituals and the Blues*, 4.

6. Cone, *Spirituals and the Blues*, 97–127.

7. Werner, *Change Is Gonna Come*, 79.

improvisations. They sought to create something new out of the feeling of the moment.

But even as Sabbath broke new ground, they drew from established blues musicians. Turning the distortion all the way up, using Wah and other effects pedals, pounding jazz rhythms on the drums, and singing trippy lyrics over blues chord patterns, were already staples of the revolutionary style of Jimi Hendrix. Hendrix was the original pioneer of heavy metal. It is not difficult to hear the musical resemblance between Hendrix and Sabbath, on songs like "Purple Haze" and "Voodoo Child." Hendrix was an international sensation in the late sixties when Sabbath was developing their sound and starting to play shows. He died on September 18, 1970, the same day Sabbath's second album, *Paranoid*, was released.[8]

Before Jimi Hendrix, there was Howlin' Wolf. Not only did Black Sabbath play Howlin' Wolf songs in their early days, but the music and themes of Howlin' Wolf can be recognized in heavy metal music from Black Sabbath to today. Hubert Sumlin's distorted guitar playing, the sinister imagery and moody tonalities, and the wicked croon of Chester Arthur Burnett set the foundations for the brooding depth of heavy metal. Listen to Sabbath's song "Black Sabbath" next to Howlin' Wolf's song "Evil." Burnett's vocal performance is as haunting as anything Ozzy sings.[9] He pronounces "evil" as though evil were a sound he could actually conjure up. Conjuring evil through sound is one of Black Sabbath's signature character traits. On "Black Sabbath," Ozzy is filled with the same dread, and he depicts an experience of evil. Both songs issue a warning:

8. See Tracy, "Hendrix, Jimi."

9. Howlin' Wolf, "Evil," written by Willie Dixon, *Moanin' in the Moonlight* (DOL, 2013).

Black Sabbath, "Black Sabbath":

> People running 'cause they're scared
> The people better go and beware

Howlin' Wolf, "Evil":

> I'm warning you brother
> You better watch your happy home

Howlin' Wolf's blues could be as heavy and foreboding as Sabbath's music, and that even in the early 1950s.

The theme of Satan—commonly associated with Sabbath and other heavy metal bands like AC/DC, Iron Maiden, and Mötley Crue—was also originally a fixture of blues music.[10] One of the earliest and greatest blues stylists, Bessie Smith, sang about the devil in "Blue Spirit Blues," which is strikingly similar to Sabbath's "Black Sabbath."[11] Both songs depict personal experiences of hell, full of the usual fire-and-brimstone imagery, but graphic in their respective expressions of it. In both songs, a sinister figure escorts them down to hell, where they begin to see flames. As they enter, devils greet them with smiles. They run and cry out in horror.

Another architect of the blues, Robert Johnson, was mythologized as the man who "went to the crossroads" to sell his soul to the devil in exchange for outstanding guitar skills.[12] While Johnson's lyrical themes included references to the devil and hell—as in songs like "Me and the Devil Blues" and "Hellhound on My Trail"—the deeper history behind the myth of his Faustian transaction is more ideological.

10. Helen Farley traces the connection between the occult in blues and the occult in heavy metal in "Demons, Devils, and Witches."

11. See Angela Davis's transcription of the song in *Blues Legacies and Black Feminism*, 294.

12. See Harmon, "Crossroads," as well as Pearson and McCulloch, *Robert Johnson*, 65–67, and Gussow, *Beyond the Crossroads*.

The crossroads myth is a remix of a myth from the Romantic period surrounding the Italian violinist Niccolo Paganini. He was said to have sold his soul to Satan in exchange for violin skills. Telling the story of this Paganini legend, the musicologist Maiko Kawabata noted that the violin was perceived in the Romantic period as a mystical, feminine instrument, "seeming to contain hidden powers waiting to be unleashed."[13] The violin had a status "as a 'magic box' whose deepest secrets could only be unlocked by the most gifted virtuosos."[14] The violinist was "an agent of death," and the violin, "a victimized, eroticized woman."[15] The subtext is that the man who can penetrate the secrets of the female body threatens the patriarchal society that seeks to dominate women. When the violin, with its curves and fluttery tones, captured feminine sexuality in the patriarchal imagination, the violinist, the one who held the reigns of this musical chaos, became a demonic figure.

The "satanic" in blues music and in rock music stems from this same hyper-sexualized hatred of femininity, as well as an insidious hatred of blackness. A black guitarist, caressing his instrument, drawing out mysterious sounds, defies gender norms, and threatens white male dominance. As the musician Gil Scott-Heron said, "White people couldn't dig having their daughters go to no shows and cream over no black man wiggling on the stage."[16] When

13. Kawabata, "Virtuosity, the Violin, the Devil," 94.

14. Kawabata, "Virtuosity, the Violin, the Devil," 94.

15. Kawabata, "Virtuosity, the Violin, the Devil," 85.

16. Gil Scott-Heron, "Ain't No New Thing," *Free Will* (Flying Dutchman Records, 1972). Sociologist Deena Weinstein similarly explains: "Rock and roll was maligned [during the 1950s] for the danger it posed inflaming the sexual passions of the [American] youth. This surface criticism masked widespread racism and fear of miscegenation. Rock and roll was believed to be infecting white youth with the supposed moral laxity of blacks. The mass media

black rhythm and blues artists started climbing the charts, it was a scandal to white men. A 1960 KKK poster read:

> Help save the youth of America
>
> DON'T BUY NEGRO RECORDS
>
> The screaming, idiotic words and savage music of these records are undermining the morals of our white youth in America.[17]

This racism is consistent with what Frantz Fanon wrote about white male fear of black men: a white father fears a black man "because in his opinion the Negro will introduce his daughter into a sexual universe for which the father does not have the key, the weapons, or the attributes."[18] Black men in the white patriarchal imagination are hyper-sexualized, "abnormal" others. "In Europe," Fanon wrote, "the black man is the symbol of Evil. . . . Satan is black."[19]

Robert Johnson became a satanic figure because he was black, because he expressed his suffering through groans and wild guitar playing, because he was talented on a revolutionary level, and because his talent had nothing to do with whiteness. The forms he came up with, his rhythms and his melodies, owed almost nothing to European standards. They were African, African American, and his own.[20]

---

responded to hat fear with the compromise of presenting white cover versions of rock-and-roll songs that had been originally recorded by blacks." Weinstein, *Heavy Metal*, 245.

17. Quoted in Weinstein, *Heavy Metal*, 245.

18. Fanon, *Black Skin, White Masks*, 127.

19. Fanon, *Black Skin, White Masks*, 145–46. In his "Montero" music video, Lil Nas X transvalues this xenophobia as he gives Satan a lap dance. Megan Thee Stallion also exploited the American fear of Satan and women's sexuality. The cover of her 2021 album *Something for Thee Hotties* features a picture of her in nothing but devil horns and a red tail.

20. See Kubik, *Africa and the Blues*, as well as Vulliamy, "Roots of

That that level of innovation and talent from a black person is possible is a fact the white founders of the United States desperately sought to deny.[21]

The story of British rock bands adopting black musical forms is a story of musicians discovering the power of black music, and trying to harness that power. George McKay outlines in his book *Circular Breathing* how black music's association with black liberation movements was part of the attraction for British musicians.[22] Consequently, British rock lyrics are often about injustice and the struggle for freedom. While that expression can be liberationist and revolutionary, it does not wipe away the realities of racism at play in their white cultural "borrowing."

When asked about her "vocal blackface," Janis Joplin remarked, "Being black for a while will make me a better white." This statement could be seen as a mark of Joplin's solidarity with black people. Having made a human connection with them through blues music, Joplin became more of an anti-racist. The interviewer Albert Goldman reflected on Joplin's response in his *New York Times* article entitled, "Why Do Whites Sing Black?" He opined that white blues singers "are not trying to pass [for black]. They are trying to save their souls"—specifically, they are trying to find "an emotional and spiritual freedom denied them by their own inherited culture."[23] This narrative is romantic, but it centers white people and white freedom. Recalling the discussion of rebellion versus revolution in the last chapter, we should be wary of justifying cultural appropriation by appealing to the supposed power of black culture to purify or redeem white

Black Music," 6–26.

21. See Ibram Kendi's discussion of Phyllis Wheatley in *Stamped from the Beginning*, 92–103.

22. McKay, *Circular Breathing*, 302–3.

23. Goldman, "Why Do Whites Sing Black?"

people. Making black liberation serve the self-actualization of white people is another form of racism.

The history of rock and heavy metal—like all of British and American history—is shot through with racism. That Rosetta Tharpe was not inducted into the rock 'n' roll Hall of Fame until 2018 says it all. As upsetting as it is to dwell on this reality, it is paramount that we acknowledge it, and ask ourselves why. If for the future we want a music industry without racism, we have to start by facing the racism that has been here all along, and which continues to shape record companies, charts, and the live of musicians today.

Toward Anti-Racist Music

During the writing of this book, Ozzy Osbourne's wife, Sharon Osbourne, left her spot on the CBS show *The Talk* after she was criticized for using racial and homophobic language during her time on the show. The spotlight fell on Sharon after she suggested on air that Megan Markle was a liar. Markle had stated in an interview with Oprah Winfrey that she faced racism as a member of the British Royal Family and was even suicidal.[24] Sharon penned an apology to the black community, saying, "I am truly sorry," and that she had let her "fear & horror of being accused of being racist take over."[25] While she apologized, Ozzy tweeted, "I can't f*cking hear you! #TeamSharon."[26] Subsequently, artist Questlove shared video footage on Instagram from the TV show *The Osbournes*, which showed Ozzy in his kitchen, and on his shelves were ceramic figures of Aunt Jemima, Mammy,

---

24. Banas, "Ozzy Osbourne Shows Support for Sharon Osbourne."

25. Kelly, "Sharon Osbourne Apologises."

26. Banas, "Ozzy Osbourne Shows Support."

Uncle Mose, and other Jim Crow-era caricatures of black people which depict them as happy to be enslaved.[27]

Minstrelsy ran in the family for Sharon, as her father, Don Arden—the notorious "Al Capone of Pop," who at one point was Black Sabbath's manager—starred in BBC's *Black & White Minstrels* TV show in the 1950s, appearing in blackface. When she was young, Sharon wrote, her brother David would put greasepaint on their faces and they would go out on the street to perform their own minstrel shows.[28]

These facts, taken together, are rather sad. They reveal the lengths to which white people go to cling to innocence, even while perpetuating racist stereotypes and refusing to listen. Whether they have done something harmful is not the concern so much as whether they can restore blamelessness.

Why are white people so afraid of being called racist? We will exceed in understanding systemic injustice, speak out and carry signs in the streets, donate to the NAACP and produce Black Lives Matter T-shirts—but our progressive values rarely seem to survive the moment when our own complicity is suggested. Imagine feeling *fear and horror* when someone suggests you said something offensive. What was Sharon trying to hold onto? What self-image was she trying to maintain if she could not bear one ounce of criticism? It is as if each critical word were a crack in a pale glass idol.

And yet, Ozzy and Sharon Osbourne's fortune, as well as Don Arden's fortune, as well as Black Sabbath's fortune, are the returns on investments in the exploitation of black lives. Every dollar earned or spent by a white person found its way into their wallet by the centuries-long course of white supremacist colonialism. There is no way for white

27. See Brown, "Mammy Jars Mock Black People."

28. Osbourne, *Extreme*, 20.

people to get off the hook, to deny responsibility. We cannot attain a "white-as-snow" record of innocence. Nor can we transcend our context and acquire a personal liberation from whiteness that places us above questions of racism. We must acknowledge the truth of ourselves and our history, and we must take responsibility for repairing the damage and righting the wrongs.

It is not enough to avoid accusations of racism. As Angela Davis said, we should be anti-racist. What have white musicians done to dismantle racism in the music industry? That question carries more weight and has more profound consequences than the merely anxious questions about guilt or innocence.

In the summer of 2020, Black Sabbath publicly supported Black Lives Matter at a time when holding up that banner was construed by many white people as support for a radical terrorist organization. They no doubt offended many of their white fans by taking that position. However, many companies have used the phrase Black Lives Matter to bolster their public image. Black Lives Matter as a slogan can be profitable for businesses trying to demonstrate that they are with it and hip. Our awareness of this reality should make us conscientious. Holding up the Black Lives Matter banner can be another way for white people to exploit black people for their own gain.

Whether a band is anti-racist does not just come down to what they are willing to say publicly. Anti-racism is an ongoing commitment, and requires critical reflection at all levels of social existence. The Beatles and The Rolling Stones can be lauded for when they credited and promoted the black artists they covered.[29] But even then,

29. Nina Simone and James Brown both expressed gratitude for the way British blues bands paid tribute to black American musicians. Simone: "[British R&B bands] give credit and respect where it

both bands often saw far more material success than their black counterparts, and often had more creative control than black artists, even when they had explicitly copied those black artists.[30] We can and should ask what lengths white groups have gone to make their industry more equitable for black people.

When it comes to racism, none of us should be concerned with exonerating ourselves, or exonerating our favorite artists. Nor should we be satisfied with mere public statements. Black people have been fettered and excluded for too long, and there is simply too much work that needs doing—as much in the music industry as anywhere else—to dismantle racism and make restitution. We cannot let ourselves be sidetracked by concern for self-image, or placated with honeyed words. Holding onto knowledge of history, and refusing to live in denial or ignore the shortcomings of even our most beloved artists and groups, we can and should ask for more.

is due, something they don't do too much at home." Quoted in Ward, *Just My Soul Responding*, 175. Brown: "[The Animals, The Kinks, The Beatles, and The Rolling Stones] had a real appreciation for where the music came from and knew more about R&B and blues than most Americans." Quoted in Werner, *Change Is Gonna Come*, 79.

30. As Craig Werner noted, "The Stones did a decent job of sharing the financial rewards with some of their sources. They consistently chose black acts to open for them on their tours. . . . Still, the elements of minstrelsy in the Stones' music are undeniable. Some of their cover versions re-create the sources almost exactly." Werner, *Change Is Gonna Come*, 87. The same can be said of many British R&B bands.

6

No More Illusions

All coming-of-age stories involve some sense of disil-lusionment. Rock and its offshoots (heavy metal, punk, etc.) have always been predominantly youth- and disillusionment-driven. In the 1950s, rock could be heard at school dances, skating rinks, and diners. In the sixties, rock was outdoor concerts, flower power, underground clubs, and musicians murdering their equipment on stage. Because rock is youth driven, it tells young peoples' stories: teenage heartbreak, unrequited affection, running away. As the youth mature, the music matures. It takes on new themes: disenchantment, deconstruction, revolution. The youth begin to realize their elders do not know what they are doing. They failed to establish a fair, harmonious world. Claiming to possess wisdom, their elders, in fact, understand little, least of all the depth of their failure. Before, youth music had been about breaking rules, living free, and having fun. But now, the situation has taken on genuine urgency. The world, the youth come to see, has been plundered and broken, and not by accident but on purpose.

This spirit of disillusionment was central to the youth movement in the 1960s, especially white American youth. Young white Americans were outraged as they discovered systemic human rights violations in their country's domestic and foreign policies. Responding to their disillusionment, many of them joined the free speech, Civil Rights, and anti-war protest movements of their era. As the black revolutionary Eldridge Cleaver observed in 1968,

> What has suddenly happened is that the white race has lost its heroes. . . . The new generation of whites, appalled by the sanguine and despicable record carved over the face of the globe by their race in the last five hundred years, are rejecting the panoply of white heroes, whose heroism consisted in erecting the inglorious edifice of colonialism and imperialism . . . rooted in the myth of white supremacy and the manifest destiny of the white race.[1]

This awakening to the realities of white supremacy (happening again in my own generation) was particularly a response to black freedom movements and the war in Vietnam. Exposed to substantial waves of black protest, learning from figures like James Baldwin, Martin Luther King Jr., Malcolm X, and Ella Baker, white young people were waking up to the legacies of slavery and imperialism. They resolved to join the oppressed in their fight for liberation. And this preferential option for the oppressed is reflected in many white rock bands of the 1960s.

The essence of rock, as Jack Black announces in the beautiful film *School of Rock*, is "sticking it to the Man"—the Man being the powers that run the world, i.e. fathers, bosses, principals, generals, wardens. Rockers surely do have a "problem with authority," but it is not exactly an

1. Cleaver, *Soul on Ice*, 68–69.

aimless tempest exploding out of nothing. Nor is it an arbitrary prejudice against just anyone in charge. There is something in rock of that quality Roland Boer calls "prophetic fury against oppressive and tyrannical rulers."[2] Sticking it to the Man is about asserting power over against the powerful. You stick it to the Man by taking the Man's categories, expectations, and standards, and utterly discarding them in favor of higher truth.

Fundamentally, rock is concerned with authentic—and, therefore, rebellious—self-expression. Matthew Niermann, in his recent book *The Humble Creative*, makes a vice out of self-expression, arguing that humility and moral uprightness are the true keys to creativity. Rock music, on the other hand, to Niermann's chagrin, is creative self-expression. It is an expression of outrage toward the status quo, toward the world the Man made. Consequently, there is not a lot humble in rock, because there is not a lot humble in rage. Rage involves a certainty of wrong. It explodes from the collision of reality contradicting morality. Rage insists things should not be as they are. Instead of resolving itself and quietly calming down, it convulses with screams and cracks.

We explored Black Sabbath's prophetic fury in the chapter on apocalyptic imagination. But something happens in the fallout from prophetic fury that affects the prophet deeply. Indictment of the present order brings unfettered imagination, but also tragic awareness of the fetters.[3] The prophets in the Bible were not enchanted but disenchanted, not charming but devastating. Prophets disengage from a fantasy world, are broken down, and are rebuilt for truth. As God said to the prophet Jeremiah,

2. Boer, *Political Grace*, 88.

3. See Heschel, *Prophets*, and Brueggemann, *Prophetic Imagination*.

"See, today I appoint you over nations and over kingdoms, to pluck up and to pull down, to destroy and to overthrow, to build and to plant" (1:10).

For this work, God made Jeremiah "a fortified city, an iron pillar, and a bronze wall, against the whole land" (1:18). The prophet is like Black Sabbath's Iron Man, who is "turned to steel" to travel time "for the future of mankind." This resemblance is no accident. Geezer Butler said "Iron Man" was inspired by the story of Jesus, whom the world passed by: "Nobody wants him / They just turn their heads."[4] Jesus' resurrection in Geezer's song is an act of vengeance:

> Now the time is here
> For Iron Man to spread fear
> Vengeance from the grave
> Kills the people he once saved

The prophet attacks the world, even if only with a vision of divine justice and judgment. The book of Revelation depicts Jesus as a warrior, but his weapon is his word: "From his mouth comes a sharp sword with which to strike down the nations" (19:21). Prophecy is violence to a violent world. It is not reassuring, it is cataclysmic. In order to make way for the beauty and glory of God's promise, prophecy must lay waste to the idols of men, and shatter the fairy tales which keep people acquiescent and indifferent.

Dream-Breaking

Prophets are "dream-breakers," to borrow Ta-Nehisi Coates's term.[5] Coates talks about dream-breaking with regard to

---

4. Aarons, "Geezer Butler."
5. Coates, *We Were Eight Years in Power*, 212, 220.

the American ideology of race. He tries to pierce through American myths of manifest destiny, innocence, and redemption, and tell the harsh truth about black experience in this country. For Coates, dream-breaking involves atheism. And there is something inherently atheistic about prophecy. As the denial and deconstruction of false gods, prophecy is functionally atheistic.

In many Black Sabbath songs, we encounter the themes of disillusionment and atheism. The band stops short of denying God, but does flirt with nihilism, as if at the edge of a cliff looking down into an abyss. In their album *Vol. 4*, Sabbath's assertive theology of retribution from "War Pigs" and from their *Master of Reality* album undergoes an evolution. As Ozzy reflects, "I'm going through changes." There are not many traces of Christian theology in *Vol. 4*. In their place, we hear the band struggling to make sense of things, wounded by discovery.

I'll never forget the first time I listened to *Vol. 4*. I was born in 1993 and grew up in an evangelical-conservative pocket of the Seattle, Washington, area, so I have no hearing-Sabbath-on-the-radio or dropping-the-needle-on-Sabbath-at-a-record-store story. Almost no one I knew listened to Black Sabbath. My dad forbade me from listening to "secular music," and even from many self-professed "Christian" rock bands. In secret, I was on an unstoppable quest of musical discovery. I snuck CDs in from the library, I downloaded albums off the internet and re-titled them so my parents would not know they were forbidden groups, and I kept a shoebox of CDs hidden under my bed. I never agreed with my dad's attitude toward music, and I never obeyed his orders. He could listen to white Christian praise all he wanted, but there was no way I was going to be satisfied with that.

About the time I was thirteen, a friend taught me how to play the opening riff for Ozzy's "Crazy Train" on the guitar, and after I learned it, I played it over and over. I kept away from listening to Ozzy because I could imagine the deep shit I would get into if my dad ever discovered the Prince of Darkness in my Walkman, but I loved playing that riff. I loved it partly because of how sinister Ozzy was. He was on the darkest shirts at Hot Topic and Spencer's Gifts. And when I heard "Crazy Train," it was clear that this was evil music. Playing the riff, I felt like I was stirring some mysterious cauldron. I played it round and round. When I left home at seventeen to go to college, my dad lost his jurisdiction over my music choices entirely, and it was only a matter of time before I discovered "War Pigs" and became a Sabbath fanatic forever.

I have often felt like I have had to compensate for all the years my dad restricted my music knowledge, and that feeling has intensified my already insatiable curiosity toward music. When I listened to Black Sabbath's album *Vol. 4*, not two minutes in I felt like I was fifteen again and my friend was showing me Led Zeppelin's "Stairway to Heaven" for the first time. The speakers were on fire. I sat speechless, eyes wide, mouth agape, in a fog of disbelief.

On the opening song, "Wheels of Confusion," Iommi bursts in with a weeping solo. There is no buildup, no "Hello, good evening," the band just bangs right in, in the middle of a guitar solo. The first note Iommi plays sounds like a shriek. When he gets to the song's main riff, I picture motorcycles and leather jackets. This is *classic* rock. And then comes Ozzy's wizard crooning, soaring above the heavy rhythm:

> Long ago I wandered through my mind
> In the land of fairy tales and stories
> Lost in happiness I knew no fears
> Innocence and love was all I knew

You can imagine Ozzy's wide-eyed gaze as he slowly utters each syllable. He sounds horrified and hypnotized, like a spooky old man warning you not to go up to Dracula's castle, even as his words signify dreamy, happy places. In an epic break, Ozzy announces, "It was an illusion!" as the band shifts to the next riff, an eerie spiral of sound. Bill Ward smashes cymbals and bangs drum heads. Bliss's ceiling has cracked and imploded.

When the verse riff comes back, the song has picked up a new quality, a sense of knowing. The second verse deconstructs the first. The same terms are used, but they are flipped. Instead of being innocent and lost in happiness, now happiness is not coming so easy, the fairy tales are not as compelling, and innocence has no meaning. The bliss was made possible only by falsehood. Again, Ozzy shrieks, "It was an illusion!" and we are thrown back into Iommi's mad guitar spiral, which this time is repeated thrice, heightening its intensity. It is as if we are being shaken, head spinning.

"Wheels of Confusion" is a spectacular expression of disillusionment. The devastation in Ozzy's voice, the ominousness of the heavy guitar and bass, the dense drum hits, and the stark clarity of the lyrics combine to punch through a convicted declaration of despair. It is rage at having been deceived by a theology of illusions.

Karl Marx famously said religion is "the opium of the people."[6] He thought religion is escapism. When reality is too harsh, we retreat into the realm of fantasy. Marx compared religion to drug abuse, because the two share the ability to suppress pain and allow people to tolerate oppressive conditions. Marx believed that if we become aware of the real problems, of the conditions which produce our distress, we will be mobilized to transform these conditions and seek "*real* happiness." Real happiness, then,

6. Marx, *Critique of Hegel's Philosophy of Law*, 175.

would organically involve the dissolution of religion, for it would entail an eradication of the conditions which made religion necessary.[7] He called religion the "sigh of the oppressed," and believed that religion would be abolished with the abolition of oppression.

Geezer Butler similarly criticizes religion in the lyrics for "Cornucopia" on *Vol. 4*:

> Too much near the truth, they say
> Keep it 'til another day
> Let them have their little game
> Delusion helps to keep them sane

In Sabbath's eyes, reality induces madness, because the truth is disappointing and oppressive. This is one of Sabbath's signature transvaluations: madness reveals what society's concept of sanity seeks to cloak. Many, if not most, people cannot handle the truth, and have compromised for a simpler, distorted lens.

The ones who tell the truth are a threat to religious peace. The religious fear the prophet. They prefer their illusions. As the prophet Isaiah said,

> [They] say to the seers, "Do not see";
> and to the prophets, "Do not prophesy to us
> what is right;
> speak to us smooth things,
> prophesy illusions." (30:10)

Black Sabbath takes on a prophetic role, shooting down people's futile attempts at fabricating a blissful world. Delusions may help to keep them sane, but this is a fragile sanity. "You're gonna go insane!" Ozzy shouts. Fantasies claim sanity where there is none, just as the prophet Jeremiah

---

7. Marx, *Critique of Hegel's Philosophy of Law*, 175.

condemned false prophets for prophesying, "'Peace, peace,' where there is no peace" (6:14).

Escapism does not just disconnect people from the truth about their world and place a veil over their reality, it alienates them from their bodies. We imagine that we are healthy, and so we neglect our health. We imagine we need nothing, and so we ask for nothing.

False prophecy and illusory happiness pervade our world, especially the world of white Americans. Today, countless white Americans are lying to themselves that there is no COVID-19 pandemic, there is no need to take safety precautions, social distance, wear a mask, or get vaccinated. There is no emergency, there is no crisis. The millions of people who have died are just numbers on a screen; they are not real, they do not matter. The only thing that matters is *me feeling happy*. And so tens of millions of human beings are fueling COVID-19 and refusing to help end a global pandemic. That is too much reality for them. They would rather escape into their private happy place.

Countless white Americans are, at the same time, lying to themselves about politics as well. They say Donald Trump did not lose the US presidential election. He was the victim of massive voter fraud. Never mind that this voter fraud claim originated with Donald Trump himself, never mind that Trump's cronies tried to prove the existence of this fraud in dozens of court cases across the country and failed. Again, the only thing that matters is *how I want my own little world to be*, not how it actually is.

The widespread prevalence of QAnon among white people in the United States is a marker of just how insane the pursuit of fantasy can become. In November of 2021, hundreds of QAnon supporters gathered in Dallas, Texas, expecting the long-deceased John F. Kennedy Jr. to reemerge and announce he will be Donald Trump's vice president.[8] He did not materialize, of course, but QAnon supporters are used to adapting to failed prophecies by now. I was personally told by a white woman after Joe Biden was announced as the winner of the 2020 election that she was "100 percent certain" the results would be corrected and Trump would be sworn in at the inauguration in January 2021. It is as if there are no facts, there is no truth, and white people can just determine what they want the truth to be if they conjure up enough certainty and force of will.

But this extremism does not just pop up out of thin air. It has emerged out of a tradition of denying reality and embracing fantasy. White American evangelicals have been training their children for decades in this work. They tell their children the world is six thousand years old, the Bible is a science textbook which reveals all the secrets of the universe, this life is only the waiting room for the next one, they will go to heaven when they die, and anyone who does not confess the same will go to hell forever. They require confession of biblical literalism and inerrancy, conformity to strictly defined gender roles, and systematic alienation from society. What is this theology but a wholesale rejection of reality?

This rejection of reality has been simmering in the evangelical mind throughout the last century, and has manifested itself today in one of the most massive cult movements of human history. Meanwhile, the politicians who have manipulated evangelicals since Nixon have been systematically destroying the earth, prolonging poverty, waging war, and defending white patriarchal supremacy. Overcoming this arrangement will require a fundamental confrontation with the illusory theology of white evangelicals. With their prophetic emphasis on disillusionment,

8. Williams and Marfin, "QAnon Supporters Gather."

Black Sabbath is especially fit for helping us navigate this confrontation.

No Heaven beyond the Grave

One early casualty of our confrontation with illusory theology will be the popular Christian belief in heaven. Belief in heaven, more often than not, keeps people from criticizing the conditions in which they live, because it leads them to defer their desires for real happiness to *the next life.* If we really do believe we will go to heaven when we die, then life on earth is merely about enduring this world to get to the next one. The sufferings of the present time are not worth comparing to the glory of heaven. If that is true, then our present conditions do not matter in the grand scheme of things—hence, why so many Christians are apathetic toward social issues. Only heaven really matters. *Will you go to heaven?* That is the decisive question. How do you get to heaven? *Believe that Jesus will take you to heaven.*

Malcolm X rejected the Christian idea of heaven because he saw in it a malevolent trick that has historically served oppressors. He said,

> [The] white man's Christian religion . . . deceived and brainwashed [the one the slavemaster called] "Negro" . . . to look for his pie in the sky, and for his heaven in the hereafter, while right here on earth the slavemaster white man enjoyed *his* heaven.[9]

It is true that many enslaved African American Christians suspended fighting for freedom, and opted instead to wait patiently for the golden home promised them in heaven.[10]

9. Malcolm X, *Autobiography of Malcolm X*, 166.
10. See Baraka, *Blues People*, 38–40.

Meanwhile, white American capitalists created heaven for themselves from the returns on their investments in the hell they created for other people. Insisting there is "no Heaven beyond the grave," Malcolm X said, "If you don't do it now, you'll never know what Heaven is."[11]

Black Sabbath echoes this criticism in many of their lyrics, particularly "War Pigs," where the rich are in power and the poor must make sacrifices to do their bidding. The lesson to be learned from this systematically designed inequality is that we must analyze who our ideas are serving. We should not be naive and assume our ideas have no relationship to the political and economic conditions surrounding us. To divorce our ideas from their context is to embrace ideological escapism.

Black Sabbath rejects escapism in no uncertain terms. They describe its awful duality: soothed mind, decaying body. As Ozzy sings in "Hand of Doom" from *Paranoid*,

> From life you escape
> Reality's black drape . . .
>
> Your mind is full of pleasure
> Your body's looking ill

While we are away in our fantasy, our bodies are suffering. The suffering may not compare to the glory of heaven—that dreamy place which exists for our minds—but neglecting the suffering will only herald more misery. Reality will always have its revenge. When we neglect our health, we invite illness. When we do not care for the earth, we doom it to destruction. When we refuse to take a stand against evil in the world, we let it reign with impunity.

11. Malcolm X, speech at Nation of Islam Temple No. 15, referenced in Payne and Payne, *Dead Are Arising*, 314.

It is precisely the utter rejection of the earth by white evangelical Christians today which makes the ongoing exploitation and destruction of the earth's resources possible. Conservative politicians and opportunist executives fight to eradicate environmental protections, sell off public land to oil companies, and perpetuate our unsustainable dependence on coal. They push these objectives despite worsening environmental conditions, ever-growing evidence of extreme climate destabilization, and worldwide outcry. All the while, they are assured support from the vast majority of white evangelical Christians. Truly James Baldwin was right when he said white Americans maintain a "striking addiction to irreality."[12]

When I think of the myth of *Walpurgisnacht*, where witches were said to ascend to mountain peaks to celebrate the beginning of spring, it pains me to reflect on how such a celebration could be demonized. We *should* be celebrating the earth, and aligning ourselves to its rhythms. The earth is sacred, and according to the book of Genesis, we are its stewards (Genesis 2:15). Care for the earth is our responsibility. If the ones caring for the earth are the witches and the ones neglecting the earth are the Bible-believers, I say it is the former who truly live according to the divine calling issued in the Bible. To use the apostle Paul's words, they "do instinctively the things of the law" and so "are a law to themselves" (Romans 2:14). There are likely more atheists today doing God's work than those who claim to believe in God.

Idolicide

Theology needs an aspect of atheism. As the theologian Katherine Sonderegger wrote, atheism witnesses to the

12. Baldwin, *Price of the Ticket*, 397.

invisibility of God.[13] "God" has become too visible, too implicated in the capricious whims of power.

In 1989, an evangelical complained in a letter to the
music magazine *Hit Parader*, "If the children of America had
a picture of God on their walls instead of photos of disgust-
ing individuals like Ozzy Osbourne, our country would be
in a much healthier state."[14] Hmm. Yeah, we could do that,
but then we would be violating the second commandment,
which explicitly prohibits making "pictures of God." (And
here I thought evangelicals wanted the ten commandments
displayed at every court in the country.)

Precisely in the spirit of the second commandment,
we must protest every attempt to abuse the name of God
for self-serving purposes. We need, as the eco-feminist
theologian Ivone Gebara says, "an atheism of overly precise
images."[15] We need prophecy, an onslaught of truth, a liberation from false gods and fantasies.

Liberation theologians listen for prophecy in the
voices of the oppressed. For James Cone, the gospel of Jesus
Christ is "the inner thrust of liberation" in the oppressed
community.[16] His theology demands freedom for the oppressed as a fundamental principle. Because of this commitment, Cone wrote that if God is an oppressor, "we had
better kill God."[17] His words are reminiscent of the words
of James Baldwin in *The Fire Next Time*: "If the concept of
God has any validity or any use, it can only be to make us
larger, freer, and more loving. If God cannot do this, then
it is time we got rid of Him."[18] This qualifier is the aspect

13. See Sonderegger, *Systematic Theology*, 52–66.

14. Quoted in Weinstein, *Heavy Metal*, 261.

15. Gebara, "Face of Transcendence," 177.

16. Cone, *Black Theology of Liberation*, 1.

17. Cone, *Black Theology of Liberation*, 28.

18. Baldwin, *Fire Next Time*, 47.

of atheism we need. Liberation theology denies any and all oppressor gods, making commitment to real freedom the litmus test for any gospel worth its salt.

Liberation theology is often criticized for making God in the image of creatures (i.e., oppressed creatures), but in truth liberation theology is the protest against false gods and the proclamation of the one true God of justice and love. The oppressor's god is always an idol. It is always used by tyrants to claim absolute authority and domination, but this is an inherently idolatrous claim. The only way to witness to God in an oppressive system is to witness to the liberation of the oppressed. Liberation theology promotes *idolicide*.

Time to Turn Away

The song which follows "Wheels of Confusion" on Black Sabbath's *Vol. 4* is called "The Straightener." It has a distinct riding-off-into-the-sunset vibe. The title suggests that the fall through the wheels of confusion resolves in a straightening up and moving along. The band elected to fade the song out instead of giving it a definitive ending. We are no longer looking backward, but forward. Yesterday's fantasies turn to "Tomorrow's Dream," the next song on the album, where Ozzy sings:

> When sadness fills my days
> It's time to turn away
> And let tomorrow's dreams
> Become reality to me

Having realized our conception has been divorced from reality, we wake up to find ourselves married to reality and in need of reconciliation with our estranged partner. Reconciliation can be found in the promise of the future. Geezer used the words "turn away"—the essence of conversion.

Conversion is a turning back from evil for reorientation toward the justice of God. While we have been devastated and disappointed by a world of lies, while we have denied reality and tried to escape into fantasy, we can change, we can turn away. The future holds the possibility of transformation.

We can see, our illusions have cost us too much, and we cannot hold to them any longer. It is only when we reject illusory pleasure that we begin to assess the real health of our bodies and of our communities. We begin to ask questions about our surroundings. We seek the welfare of the world in which live. After all, this world is all we have. This is the earth with which God has graced us. As I read on a street post in Bed Stuy, "There is no Planet B." This is where we must have heaven.

7

Deep Things of Satan

The figure of Satan is everywhere in Black Sabbath's music. Even in their first album, Satan showed up in the band's namesake song, as well as in "N.I.B."[1] where "Lucifer" is the subject. Ozzy Osbourne and Tony Iommi have downplayed their early satanic themes (due to the "satanic panic" surrounding their music), but just like Led Zeppelin, Black Sabbath was influenced by the occult, particularly the work of Aleister Crowley.[2] In an interview, Geezer cited Crowley as a significant influence on his intellectual development from devout Catholic to apostate with an affinity for occult-Satanist literature. Sabbath was also the band that popularized the devil horns hand gesture that people throw up at concerts to signal, "Rock on!" Ozzy would eventually release "Mr. Crowley" on his first solo album *Blizzard of Ozz*, a song which is addressed to Crowley and searches his life and teaching.[3] While the

1. In Sabbath lore, "N.I.B." means "Nativity in Black."
2. See Cope, "Dichotomy of Aesthetics."
3. Butler: "I'd been raised a Catholic so I totally believed in the Devil. There was a weekly magazine entitled 'Man, Myth And Magic'

sensationalist theories about supposed subliminal messages and backmasking in certain heavy metal songs are
nonsense, it is true that early British heavy metal bands
were to some extent explicitly Satanist.

Jimmy Page from Led Zeppelin had the words "Do
what thou wilt" engraved on the vinyl of *Led Zeppelin III*—
the words which constitute "the whole of the law" according to Thelema, Aleister Crowley's religion.[4] The lifestyle
heavy metal musicians led is not inconsequential to the
Satanism in which they dabbled. "Sex, drugs, and rock 'n'
roll," it turns out, is Satanist. But what Satanism constitutes
and who Satan is, are far from simple.

The question I wish to explore in this chapter is
whether Black Sabbath's proximity to Satanism is such a
bad thing. Is it possible for theologians to read Satan with
charity? How does Black Sabbath witness to Satan theologically? Tackling these questions will require exploring Aleister Crowley's Satanism and Sabbath's divergent reception of
it. I will then compare Black Sabbath's depiction of Satan to
the Satan in the Bible, tracing the evolution of Satan from
the Old Testament to the Dead Sea Scrolls to the New Testament. I will produce not just a kinship between the biblical
Satan and Sabbath's, but a reconstruction of Satanology that
affords Satan a *godly* role in the apocalyptic theology I have
been outlining with Black Sabbath.

---

that I started reading which was all about Satan and stuff. That and
the books by Aleister Crowley and Dennis Wheatley, especially 'The
Devil Rides Out' which was meant to be a cautionary tale but which
read like a handbook on how to be a Satanist." Quoted in Black Sabbath, *Reunion*, CD (Epic, 1998), liner notes.

4. See Crowley, *Book of the Law*, 9.

Satan in Black Sabbath

There have been many forms of Satanism over the years. The secular humanist Satanic Temple of today, for example, is an altogether different phenomenon from Crowley's Satanism. Crowley was notoriously hedonistic, believing that it is right to be led, with reckless abandon, by one's desires. "Do what thou wilt" is the mantra of the libertine who consumes all he wants. Black Sabbath exhibited this do-what-thou-wilt spirit in the lives they led—spending eye-popping lengths of time on and off tour getting sloshed, snorting coke, and shagging groupies. Yet, in their lyrics, Sabbath admitted a criticism of their own habits and an awareness of the limitations of Thelemic libertarianism. Ozzy, in his song on Crowley, called Crowley's lifestyle "tragic," even while he saw "the thrill of it all."

"The Thrill of It All" is also the name of a song from Sabbath's album *Sabotage*. The title is a reference to Crowley's writings, especially the *Rites of Eleusis*, which Crowley intended would guide participants to a state of ecstasy, to experience a euphoric "thrill."[5] Crowley's Satan is like Dionysus, the god of intoxication.[6] Dionysus (or "Bacchus") is often pictured with arms stretched wide, one hand holding up a cup of wine, the other full of fruit; he embraces all things, and beckons for divine nectar. "I'll fathom the bowl!" as the old English drinking song goes. Crowley's Satanism is Dionysian self-indulgence, and Black Sabbath reflects this pursuit of pleasure and ecstasy.

With their music, Black Sabbath essentially modeled Crowley's magic acts. Every Sabbath performance is a magic act and occasion for ecstasy. As Ozzy stated in an interview, the way movies can act out horror for an

5. Tupman, "Theatre Magick."

6. On Dionysus, see Nietzsche, *Birth of Tragedy*, 14–19.

audience, Ozzy acts out horror in his music and on stage.[7] He sings on "Mr. Crowley," "You fooled all the people with magic / Yeah, you waited on Satan's call." To follow Satan's call means to develop the art of astonishment. Sabbath-Crowley Satanism is a grand show designed to inspire awe and euphoria in the audience.

The Sabbath musicians, however, did not directly engage in Satan worship or occult practice. Iommi and Ozzy wrote in their autobiographies about attracting a following of Satanists in their early years, but these groups grew disenchanted with Sabbath when it was clear the band was not serious about the occult or would not participate in their ceremonies. All four Sabbath members started wearing crucifixes around their necks after an apparent Satanist group put a curse on them when the band refused an invitation. It is their habit to this day. Iommi says in his autobiography, "We all had this dream about wearing crosses to protect us from evil. And so we did. . . . I never go on stage without wearing my cross."[8] On Iommi's Signature Epiphone SG, crosses are figured up and down the fretboard. The irony that Black Sabbath had an inverted cross in the sleeve of their first album and crucifixes around their necks is not an accident. This combination witnesses to the contrasts Sabbath repeatedly elected to portray. As Iommi described in his autobiography, he is always looking for "light and shade" in his creative process.[9]

Crowley's *Book of the Law* proclaims, "Do what thou wilt shall be the *whole* of the law," but Sabbath's lyrics consistently reject the choice to follow one's own will over against the will of wisdom. In their flag-ship song, Sabbath announced the doom of the self-willed individual: "Turn

7. See Rare Metal Videos, "Rare Ozzy Osbourne Video."

8. Iommi, *Iron Man*, 81–82.

9. Iommi, *Iron Man*, 133.

'round quick and start to run / Find out I'm the chosen one." Their song "Hand of Doom" begins with the words, "Watcha gonna do? / Time's caught up with you." On "Wheels of Confusion," Ozzy declares, "Try your hardest, you'll still be a loser / The world will still be turning when you're gone." Throughout their music, Black Sabbath intimates that humans are not reliable, that we have a tendency to alienate ourselves from ourselves and from our world, and that we are in need of learning how to do better. We cannot simply commit to doing whatever we want to do. As Ozzy sings in "Fairies Wear Boots," "I went to the doctor, see what he could give me / He said, son, son you've gone too far." Geezer in his lyrics displays a preference for self-awareness and self-criticism, which precludes the idea that we should forget ourselves in ecstatic self-indulgence.

Geezer Butler's experience with a fire-and-brimstone missionary during his coming of age had led him to ask, "If that is what God is like, what is Satan like?" He pursued occult literature out of that interest, but ultimately rejected Satanism. He described this rejection in an interview from the 2010s where he recounted an experience he thought was an encounter with Satan. Laying in bed, surrounded by inverted crosses and pictures of the devil on the black walls of his flat, Butler woke up to see a "black shape" standing at the end of his bed. He interpreted this visitation as an ultimatum: "It's time to either pledge allegiance or piss off!" From then on, according to Butler, "I just went off the whole thing."[10]

It is possible Butler overstates this turning point and downplays the role of Satan in his early Sabbath lyrics. While it is true that his lyrics became less satanic as time went on, Geezer wrote the lyrics for "Black Sabbath," "War Pigs," and "N.I.B." *after* his turning-point experience,

10. Butler, quoted in Wall, *Black Sabbath*, 40.

and was in fact partly inspired by it. The "black shape" he spoke of shows up at the opening of "Black Sabbath." Further, "N.I.B." is written from Satan's point of view, and confesses, "The sun, the moon, the stars all bear my seal." And the original lyrics to "War Pigs" were quite different and featured more satanic themes.

"War Pigs" was originally called "Walpurgis," which comes from Walpurgis Night. In German folklore, it is the night before May 1st when witches would meet for spring ceremonies in the Harz Mountains.[11] Walpurgis Night shows up in Aleister Crowley's *Moonchild*, as well as J. S. Goethe's *Faust* and Bram Stoker's *Dracula's Guest*.[12] When the producers at Vertigo Records heard the song, they said it was too satanic.[13] Indeed, the lyrics of "Walpurgis" are more graphic and hellish than those heard on *Paranoid*. We can hear them on bootleg recordings of early Sabbath concerts.[14] The beginning lines alone signal different scenes:

War Pigs:

> Generals gathered in their masses
> Just like witches at black masses

Walpurgis:

> Witches gathered at black masses
> Bodies burning in red ashes

"War Pigs" uses the black mass as a symbol of generals waging war, as a critique of the military-industrial complex. "Walpurgis," on the other hand, describes a terrifying black mass,

11. Knowles, *ODPF*, s.v. "Walpurgis Night."

12. Froese, "Black Sabbath's Apocalypse of Horror," 24.

13. Stolz, *Experiencing Black Sabbath*, 11.

14. See HDBlackSabbath, "Black Sabbath—Live at the Audimax," as well as The Hellfire God, "Black Sabbath—Walpurgis Remastered 1970."

where people are tortured, churches are destroyed, sinners eat rats, and the devil is in charge. Throughout "Walpurgis," Geezer deployed the Christian category of the sinner, but he granted the devil the lordship usually reserved for God. In the book of Revelation, God casts the devil into fire (Rev 20:10); in "Walpurgis," Satan is doing the casting. A priest appears, hell's inhabitants flock to him, but Satan promptly tosses him in the flames. "It's the same wherever you may go / To black masses people go," Ozzy sings, announcing Satan's universal lordship. These lyrics are repeated at the conclusion of the song: "wherever you may go." *All* are ultimately subject to the power of the devil.

The same conclusion can be found on the bootlegs of the original "Black Sabbath" song from 1970. When their self-titled album debuted, the titular song was released without its final verse. While consistent with the rest of the song, the extra verse reveals a graphic, unhappy ending:

> Child cries out for his mother
> Mother screaming in the fire
> Satan points at me again
> Opens the door to push me in[15]

When I heard these lyrics on a recording for the first time, I was shaken, much like the audience was shaken. According to the band, early in their career, when they would finish performing their original songs, the audience would not clap or shout but were dead silent, hypnotized, maybe even scandalized. The original lyrics to "War Pigs" and "Black Sabbath" stand out as more gruesome and shocking than what is heard on the album.

In the revised lyrics of "War Pigs," however, Satan exists not in place of God but side-by-side with God. God metes out justice and Satan enjoys it: "Hand of God has

15. HDBlackSabbath, "Black Sabbath—Live at the Audimax."

struck the hour / . . . Satan laughing spreads his wings." This new angle on Satan anticipates his appearance in *Master of Reality*. In the song "Lord of This World," Satan says,

> Your world was made for you by someone above
> But you chose evil ways instead of love
> You made me master of the world where you exist
> The soul I took from you was not even missed

In the Bible, Satan is called "the ruler of this world" (John 12:31; 14:30; 16:11), "the god of this world" (2 Corinthians 4:4), and "the ruler of the power of the air" (Ephesians 2:2). First John 5:49 says, "The whole world is under the control of the evil one." Black Sabbath shares this bleak outlook, referring to Satan as "master of the world." And yet, here Satan witnesses to God's truth. "Your world was made for you by someone above," whose ways are defined by love and not evil. Satan, even in his opposition to God, serves God. Black Sabbath envisions Satan as the executor of the human will toward evil. Satan delivers the consequences of evil actions, and relishes the recompense.

Sabbath's engagement with Satan is unique because it is balanced by a commitment to Christian ideas. The dialectical tension between God and Satan in Geezer Butler's lyrics creates a vision of a world in contradiction and struggle—good and evil, heaven and hell, cross and inverted cross. And yet, even in the song "Walpurgis," Satan is not responsible for evil; rather, he executes the wrath of justice. Ozzy sings the word "sinners" three times. The song's conceit is that the unfortunate people in hell deserve their punishment, that they have freely given themselves over to Satan's lordship.

While it may seem transgressive or fiendish that Black Sabbath rocks out to a priest being throne into hellfire, we are also aware that priests are not exactly the group we can most count on to be good. The history of corrupt and hypocritical priests is as long as the history of priesthood. The bitter irony is that those who have been entrusted to represent Jesus and minister to peoples' needs are often among the most despicable we could describe. Geezer alludes to being disillusioned by priests in his lyrics. On "Sabbath Bloody Sabbath," Ozzy bemoans those who "fill your head all full of lies." On "Lord of This World," he prophesies doom for hypocrites who claim to be pure but are arrogant and greedy: "Lord of this world / Evil possessor / Lord of this world / He's your confessor now."

Black Sabbath clearly enjoys pronouncing this judgment, and enjoys identifying with Satan the prosecutor. On "Black Sabbath" and "War Pigs," Satan smiles and laughs as those who sowed violence and injustice on the earth reap God's judgment. There is a medieval spirit to Sabbath's theology. If we make the wrong choices, we will end up in Satan's clutches, and he will enjoy witnessing our comeuppance. In this way, Black Sabbath outlines Satan's place within God's providence.

In Sabbath's music, Satan witnesses to divine justice, even as he is assumed to be God's enemy. Inversely, the priests betray their vocation and blaspheme the name of God. It is a topsy-turvy world. The church, the realm of God, is full of hypocrisy; and the world, the realm of Satan, fails to prove entirely evil. It is as if heaven betrays its goodness, hell betrays its evil, and this dynamic determines life on earth.

Satan in the Bible

Black Sabbath's depiction of Satan is not too far off from depictions of Satan in the Bible—especially the book of Job and the book of Revelation. In Job—one of the earliest

biblical texts that mention Satan—Satan is not a personifi-
cation of evil, but an active agent in God's court. The name
"Satan" comes from the Hebrew word *hasatan*, which is not
a name but a noun meaning "the adversary."[16] *Hasatan* (the
satan) in Job is not an evil figure but a clever, suspicious
one.[17] He is not God's enemy, but also not quite a member
of God's inner circle. He roams "to and fro on the earth"
(1:7). He is like a freelance agent, the sole member of a
specialized task force. His job is to be skeptical, to distrust
what he sees, to ask questions.

When God says to him that Job is "blameless and upright," Satan asks the crucial question: "Does Job fear God
for nothing?" (1:8–9). There is no malevolence in this question. He has simply made a connection between Job's prosperity and the uprightness of Job's character. Satan followed
the money. Job can *afford* to be good, but how do we know
he is *genuine*? Satan does not buy into the façade. "Stretch
out your hand now," he tells God, "and touch all that he
has, and he will curse you to your face" (Job 1:11). In other
words, threaten to take Job's wealth or power, and, Satan
thinks, we will see a whole new side of Job.

The hilarious thing is that God agrees! "Very well," he
says (1:12). Where is the God of classical philosophy who
knows all things and undergoes no change or affection?
Does God *not know* whether Job is genuine? Apparently
not, for God does not trust Job either. In fact, it is God
who initiated the conversation—"Have you considered my
servant Job?" (1:8). We might think at first God is brag-
ging when Job is called "blameless and upright," but now
it seems the conversation was initiated because God was

16. Alter, *Job*, 12.

17. See Day, *Adversary in Heaven*, and Wray and Mobley, *Birth
of Satan*.

suspicious of Mr. 500 Donkeys—Job, "the greatest of all the people of the east" (v. 3).

Suddenly Job has not a friend in the world. Neither Satan nor God trusts his goodness. If Job knew of this conversation, he would doubtless be horrified to find he was made destitute and miserable because God and Satan decided he was too good to be true. But then again, perhaps God and Satan know something Job does not. They know the correspondence between wealth and nobility, and they are united in distrust of the affluent. Their relationship here is similar to the way God and Satan are portrayed together in "War Pigs"—on the same team, Satan working alongside God to test the limits of human integrity and try the accused.

Jesus in the New Testament had to face the same test Job faced. In the Gospel of Matthew, Satan tries to get Jesus to defy God, in exchange for "all the kingdoms of the world" (4:8). Satan offers to make Jesus rich and prosperous, like Job. In this story, Satan again is testing the limits of human righteousness. But by the time Matthew was written, the character of Satan had gone through a transformation. As ideas had circulated in the ancient Near East, Satan developed from an adversary to an evil being—as he is in the book of Enoch from the Dead Sea Scrolls.[18]

In 1 Enoch, a fallen angel named Azazel leads a band of angels, or "Watchers," on a journey to earth to copulate with human women. This story is a nod to the book of Genesis in the Hebrew Bible, which says that at the origin of civilization, angels, called *nephilim*, came down to earth and "went in to the daughters of humans" (6:4). *Nephilim*

18. The Dead Sea Scrolls are texts from Jewish sects of the Greco-Roman world which can generally be dated from the second century BCE to the first century CE, making them close to the time of Jesus. See Collins, *Dead Sea Scrolls*, and Vermes, *Complete Dead Sea Scrolls in English*.

in Hebrew means "fallen ones."[19] In the 1 Enoch version, when these fallen angels mated with human women, they created demonic beings who proceeded to wreak havoc and destruction all over the earth. Azazel, who is called "Satan" later in the book, is thereby responsible for all evil.[20] This story is also the precursor of the myth of the "black sabbath," where Satan and his demons mate with human witches and conceive evil beings.[21]

The wildness of *hasatan* in Job—that he wanders to and fro, that he exists somehow apart from God, that he is an adversary—morphed over time into a monstrous, supreme antagonism. By the first century CE, Jesus and his followers shared the apocalyptic dualism of Enoch and other texts from the Dead Sea Scrolls. They did not see Satan as God's resident skeptic, but, rather, as "the Evil One" (1 John 5:19), "the father of lies" (John 8:44), "the deceiver of the whole world" (Revelation 12:9). While early Christians still believed that Satan tests human uprightness, they condemned Satan's work as "temptation." They considered Satan responsible for exposing people to evil and tricking them into following it. Later generations of Christians fleshed this idea out and through their imaginations produced the grisly images of a blood red, goat-horned devil engulfed in darkness, flames, and the screams of his victims.

I do not believe this Satan is real. I do not believe there is a supernatural creature working mischievously behind history to create weal and make woe. And I contend that these fantasies of demons and diabolical beings keep us from reflecting on the causes of our struggles right in

---

19. Alter, *Genesis*, 27.

20. See Wray and Mobley, *Birth of Satan*, 95–112. On 1 Enoch, see Charlesworth, *OTP*, 5–89.

21. Wray and Mobley, *Birth of Satan*, 102.

front of us. The real enemies are in our midst. And I do not think the secret to their tyranny lies in some super-sensible hell. Rather, I believe evil functions in the human structures which we ourselves have developed over time.

In the book of Isaiah, the prophet judges oppressive world leaders, announcing their coming destruction. In one poem, he literally taunts King Nebuchadnezzar II of Babylon, who had met an untimely end:

> How are you fallen from heaven,
>   O Day Star, son of Dawn! . . .
> You said in your heart,
>   "I will ascend to heaven;
> I will raise my throne
>   above the stars of God. . . .
> But you are brought down to Sheol,
>   to the depths of the Pit." (14:12–15)

Sheol/Pit are the closest Hebrew equivalents to our word "hell," and "Day Star" translated to Greek is *lucifer*. Isaiah used this term to make fun of Nebuchadnezzar II. He shined so bright and ascended great heights, only to fall to deprivation and disgrace.[22] As the author(s) of the book of Enoch developed their Satanology, they drew from this reference in Isaiah. The image of a shining star plunging into darkness, combined with the image of the fallen angel who wreaks havoc on the earth, accounts for our understanding of Lucifer today.

---

22. It is likely the writer drew inspiration from an ancient Canaanite myth in which the god Athtar, who was associated with the planet Venus (referred to as the "Day Star" because it could be seen in the morning), ascended to the throne of God but because of his arrogance was demoted to lord of the Underworld. See Heiser, "Mythological Provenance of Isaiah XIV 12–15."

Originally, however, Lucifer was not a supernatural figure, but a name given to a tyrant in our midst. King Nebuchadnezzar II in the sixth century BCE laid siege to Jerusalem, forced Israelites into exile from their land, and held them captive in Babylon. Isaiah prophesied the destruction of Nebuchadnezzar's empire, and not only his empire, but all empires that are maintained through violence and injustice:

> See, the day of the Lord comes,
>
>> cruel, with wrath and fierce anger. . . .
>
> The stars of the heavens . . . will not give their light;
>
>> the sun will be dark at its rising. . . .
>
> I will put an end to the pride of the arrogant,
>
>> and lay low the insolence of tyrants. (13:9–11)

Isaiah prophesied that God overthrows oppressors and liberates the oppressed, for this is divine justice.[23]

When the New Testament refers to Satan, its implications are similarly aimed at oppressive imperial powers. For example, when Paul says "the god of this world" acts to keep people from seeing "Christ, who is the image of God," his Roman-imperial context should be kept in mind. Caesar had deemed himself god and lord, and expected his subjects to worship him as such. When Paul said Christ is "the image of God," he was undermining Caesar's claim to lordship and denying his right to be worshipped and obeyed.[24] Jesus is "King of kings and Lord of lords" (Revelation 19:16). The loyalty demanded of Christ-followers ruled out submission to Caesar. Whatever the pharaoh, the caesar, the king, the president claims for himself, God trumps all.

When Jesus said, "Render to Caesar what is Caesar's and to God what is God's," the subtext is, render to

23. Compare Isa 14:12–15 with 13:9–11; and 14:3–6 with 61:1–2.

24. See Maier, *New Testament Christianity*, 83–94.

God everything and Caesar nothing, for nothing belongs to Caesar which does not ultimately belong to God. As the book of Deuteronomy in the Hebrew Bible says, "To the Lord your God belong the heavens, even the highest heavens, the earth and everything in it" (10:14). Biblical theology thus harbors the potential for rebellion, revolution, and tyrannicide. It was for this reason Rome had Jesus killed. The Roman authorities felt threatened by the fact that Jesus' disciples called him king, and feared he would inspire a revolution.[25] In the same way that J. Edgar Hoover feared Fred Hampton, Caesar feared Jesus. In light of this context, Paul's reference to "the god of this world" is a satirical nod to Caesar's big lie.

The same is true of the way Satan is used in the book of Revelation. Biblical scholar Elisabeth Schüssler Fiorenza contends that the dragon, and the beasts the dragon summons, symbolize Rome, Caesar, and the evil forces at work in them.[26] Writing to Christians in Asia minor, the author of Revelation declared that those who "buy or sell" in an exploitative economy, or participate in the idolatry of the imperial cult, carry "the mark of the beast" (Revelation 13:17). They help form the incessant, interlocking web of imperial power. In this context, Satan represents the overall conspiracy and deception that maintain that power.

The Morning Star

We have come a long way from the adversary character in the book of Job. In the New Testament, Satan is not just "an auditor of human virtue,"[27] he is the arch-oppressor, the

25. See Horsley, "Jesus and Empire," 75.
26. Schüssler Fiorenza, *Book of Revelation*, 75.
27. Wray and Mobley, *Birth of Satan*, 58–64.

deceiver, the Evil One. So we see Satan is depicted in the Bible in various ways. Black Sabbath, too, is comfortable depicting diverse notions of Satan. Satan is both a diabolical overlord and a cunning prosecutor. In the move from "Walpurgis" to "War Pigs," Sabbath used one Satan to undermine the other. Satan the adversary executes God's wrath against Satan the tyrant. And, indeed, we need a good adversary to help question our character and challenge the status quo. The Satan in God's court does not serve evil but good, insofar as he indicts oppressive powers and cuts down the arrogant. This Satan serves the good by questioning whether our status quo measures up to it. He also reminds us that human actions do genuinely have consequences.

The idea of a good Satan might strike some as ridiculous, but just as Satan is Lucifer, the "morning star," Jesus is also referred to in Revelation by this name: "It is I, Jesus, . . . I am the root and the descendant of David, the bright morning star" (Revelation 22:16). The morning star in ancient times was Venus, which appeared at dawn and was thus, "the herald of a new day."[28] The word "apocalypse" means revelation, an unveiling of things which were hidden, a tearing down of old appearances in favor of new understanding and clarity.[29] That Jesus inaugurates a new day is a universally recognized aspect of New Testament theology. Less expected, but nonetheless intriguing, is the possibility that Lucifer could signify a new dawn in the same positive sense.[30]

28. Aune, *Revelation 1–5*, 212.

29. See Hanson, "Apocalypse and Apocalypticism," 279–80.

30. For a creative engagement with Lucifer as the morning star that also pays tribute to doom metal's connection to the blues, listen to "Morning Star" by King Woman, off their 2021 album *Celestial Blues*.

Pagan Altar, an English doom metal band from the late 1970s, made just this move on their album *Judgment of the Dead*. In their song "Pagan Altar," the leader singer Terry Jones sings,

> Dawning of a brand new day
> Lighting up the way
> With something new to say
> From beyond the stars

Borrowing imagery from the book of Revelation, in the song "Judgment of the Dead," Jones sings,

> A courtroom filled with the dead
> Judge Satan sits at their head
> A cloak of black, that hangs to the ground
> Sentence is passed without even a sound

"Pagan Altar" incorporates the apocalyptic idea of the day of judgment, but swaps God for Satan. This reversal, the band intimates, is necessitated by the hypocrisy and corruption they see in organized religion. Echoing Black Sabbath's "War Pigs," Jones goes on to sing:

> Politicians standing in line
> Generals following behind
> Chained to the dock with the leaders of religion,
> Heads bowed low awaiting the decision

Here is apocalyptic imagination which, like the book of Revelation, stands for justice and the dawning of a new day without corruption or evil. Only, instead of Jesus Christ, we get Satan. But the thrust of the vision still carries. Those who destroy the earth will be destroyed, and this will be the dawn of a brand new day. Jesus and Satan join together in a vision of divine apocalypse, and the name they both bear is "morning star."

8

God Is the Only Way to Love

Whoever loves has been born of God and knows God. Anyone who does not love does not know God, because God is Love.

—1 John 4:7–8

Love that does not satisfy justice is no love at all. It is merely a sentimental affection, little more than what one would have for a pet.

—Dr. Martin Luther King Jr.

Revolution in their minds the children start to march . . .

They'll fight the world until they've won

And love comes flowing through

—Geezer Butler of Black Sabbath

"This ain't the summer of love," Blue Öyster Cult announced on a song from 1976, while rejecting images like "angels" and "the garden of Eden." The band was following the lead of Black Sabbath, who, as Iommi wrote in his memoir, rejected "flower power" and all the "nice and happy" themes that showed up in much of the music of the 1960s. Sabbath wanted to talk about "real life," about the realities people did not want to acknowledge.

I began this book by highlighting Sabbath's bleak perspective of the world as evil, a providence of sorrow. There seemed to be no place for love in Sabbath's world. But that is not the whole story. There is another thread that runs through Sabbath's signature albums, hidden in the heavy music and shrill vocals. Even as they embody the world's bleakness, Sabbath sneaks in intimations of the supremacy of love. In this chapter, I will explore Black Sabbath's theology of love, and how it squares with their heavy metal outlook and their complicated history.

Confronting Xenophobia in Metal Subculture

We will get to Black Sabbath's theology of love, but first we need to ask some questions about the antipathy toward love that Sabbath seems to harbor. What was it that Sabbath had against flower power? What does Sabbath stand for that is incompatible with centering love? Is there something *unloving* about Black Sabbath? Asking these questions will bring to the fore some unfortunate and disagreeable elements of metal subculture which have existed since its inception and development, and it would be irresponsible to talk about metal and love without critically examining these elements.

For most of Black Sabbath's career, their music has been enjoyed predominantly by straight white men. However the band members themselves conceived it, the aggression in their music appealed to young whites who were frustrated with the social upheaval that brought women, LGBT folks, and people of color at the forefront. As Deena Weinstein recounted, "Nostalgia for centricity" played a part in the development of metal subculture.[1]

In 1958, as West London's Notting Hill saw an influx of Indian and Caribbean immigrants, British "Teddy Boys," made up mostly of white men from nationalist groups like the Union Movement—whose slogan was "Keep Britain White"—roamed the city attacking people of color in riots that lasted for days. Twenty-one years later, in Chicago, thousands of young white men started a riot at Comiskey Park, the White Sox baseball stadium, burning disco and other records by black artists and chanting, "Disco sucks!" This eruption of violence was a reaction to the disco music and culture that was booming at the time, and was enjoyed primarily by black, latinx, and gay communities. In between these two events, Black Sabbath emerged as a vigorous new force in music, and captured the imagination of countless young white men who had grown nihilistic and disgusted with the world they inhabited.

This white male resentment is not unrelated to the metal aversion to the concept of love. Where love binds people together in a spirit of global community ("People of the world / Join hands / Start a love train," as The O'Jays sang in 1972), metal culture has a tendency to take pride in the idea of the lone wolf, the individual who stands apart and resists fellow-feeling and cooperation. "I just believe in myself, 'cause no one else is true," as Ozzy sings on Black Sabbath's "Under the Sun."

1. Weinstein, *Heavy Metal*, 101.

Metal individualism privileges straight white men, and harbors a homophobic and sexist emphasis on machismo and power.[2] Ozzy tweeting "I can't fucking hear you! #TeamSharon" after his wife was called out for racist comments is a good example of this tendency toward white male chauvinism. Similarly, songs like Sabbath's "Gypsy" and "Dirty Women" betray a degeneracy of spirit as they carelessly deploy racist and sexist tropes that objectify and exoticize the white man's others. Many albums by other metal groups do the same.[3]

While Black Sabbath subverts gender norms in a myriad of ways, they also, as Bill Ward said, offered "an aggressive message," one of nonconformity and resistance to societal pressures.[4] This countercultural spirit of resistance is crucial to the music, as well as to their revolutionary character, and it contributes to Sabbath's lasting power. But resistance to societal pressures becomes a pitfall when it morphs into resistance to the common good, resistance to responsibility, and resistance to otherness.

Thankfully, today, metal music is not the province of straight white men that it once was. Birmingham, England's own Rob Halford of Judas Priest came out as gay in the 1990s, and bands like Vile Creature, GRLwood, Dominatrix, G.L.O.S.S., and many others are reappropriating homophobic and sexist stereotypes, and directing metal aggression and anger toward white supremacist capitalist patriarchy. Author Margaret Killjoy and her band Feminazgûl are intentionally feminist and anti-fascist, seeking to use their music to waken social consciousness. In 2017, Danica Roem became the first trans woman to be elected to a US state legislature, and even at the time of her run for

2. See Weinstein, *Heavy Metal*, 100.

3. See Walser, *Running with the Devil*.

4. Ward, "Black Sabbath Drummer Bill Ward."

office she was the lead singer of the thrash metal band Cab Ride Home. The metal compilations *Grind against Trump* (2017), *Riffs for Reproductive Justice* (2019), and *Shut It Down* (2020) raised thousands of dollars for the Southern Poverty Law Center, the National Network of Abortion Funds, and the Movement for Black Lives, respectively, demonstrating what metal bands can come together to accomplish toward justice. Many, if not all, of these artists draw inspiration from Black Sabbath, seeing in their music and lyrics a prophetic cry for liberation.

To state the obvious, metal should not be about lashing out at the inclusion of people who are different from you. But even setting aside the moral question, chauvinism contradicts the original spirit of metal music. Ozzy's howling, Bill Ward's pounding, Iommi's slashing, Geezer's booming; these explosions of sound, of dread and of pain—this is the cry of the earth over the destruction of life. Black Sabbath's music was born of the ruins of war and the depression of poverty. They witnessed a world in agony, bursting with rage, and they felt their own agony and rage with it. They expressed the world's disharmony through creative rebellion, and they tapped into prophetic insight: love *should* define existence.

Black Sabbath, even at their most cynical, express a longing for a world defined by love. When they focus on death, oppression, and sorrow, they confront those depths of reality which most contradict love. They shine a light on injustice. And it is from that place that they develop a theology.

Love Is Life

Black Sabbath's use of the word "love" can be divided into two senses: first, love can be a pacifying escape from reality into sentimental feeling; and second, love is the very ground of life, and the inherent hope of the world.

Sabbath is first cynical toward love, because of its hypnotic, spellbinding power. As Buddy Holly exemplified in his classic song "Words of Love," "Tell me love is real / . . . Let me hear you say / The words I long to hear." The words "tell me" betray an indifference to truth. Don't tell me the truth, just tell me what I *want* to hear. Fleetwood Mac puts it more candidly: "Tell me lies, tell me sweet little lies." Black Sabbath resents this power of love to delude people into rejecting reality. Instead of joining the choruses of the 1960s hits that endlessly praised love, in Sabbath's own hit song "Paranoid," a tortured Ozzy cries, "Love to me is so unreal."

Sabbath often depicts love as a retreat from the real world, as in "Symptom of the Universe":

> Take my hand and we'll go riding through the sunshine from above
>
> We'll find happiness together in the summer skies of love

The concept of love here is illustrated in the image of riding off in the sunset happily ever after, like the producers' cut of an auteur director's esoteric film.[5] It is natural to want to imagine that love wins, that no obstacle is too threatening for ol' irresistible love. Love bears a promise which is too painful to relinquish, even if it means the fulfillment of the promise can only occur in a fantasy. So love, Sabbath complains, is often too fantastical, the stuff

5. Ridley Scott's *Blade Runner* and Terry Gilliam's *Brazil* both originally had mysterious or tragic endings, and they were hijacked and recut by their producers, who feared the lack of a happy ending would kill ticket sales. Both films were released in theaters with alternate endings where the characters literally drive off into a sunset.

of dreams and not of real life. It is sentimental, and metal is decidedly unsentimental.

This unsentimental worldview can then lead to individualism and noncooperation, wherein we deny the supremacy of love and assume the supremacy of our individual selves. Sabbath does at times display this tendency, but ultimately they issue a pronouncement against it. Individualism, too, falls under Sabbath's condemnation of the human's futile attempts to escape reality. "Try your hardest, you'll still be a loser," Ozzy states frankly on "Wheels of Confusion," and continues, "The world will still be turning when you're gone." I am not ultimate or essential. In my finite being, I am already usurped by the vast universe beyond me. Clearly, something more is needed than simple faith in myself.

Perhaps the most surprising Black Sabbath song in existence is "After Forever," from *Master of Reality*, which can genuinely be regarded as the first Christian metal song. Geezer Butler's use of Christian theology in the song's lyrics is far from subtle, complicating the band's satanic, irreligious image.

> Could it be you're afraid of what your friends
> might say
> If they knew you believe in God above?
> They should realize before they criticize
> That God is the only way to love

These words are astounding given Sabbath's reputation. Ozzy Osbourne, the Prince of Darkness himself, is actually heard on the record confessing belief in God and faith that God is "the only one who can save you now from all this sin and hate." But of course, this is no ordinary Christian theology, for none of the band members, including Geezer, profess to be Christians. It would be a mistake to read a traditional Christian theology into this song's lyrics.[6]

"God is the only way to love" is a surprisingly original theological statement, and must be read on its own terms, keeping in mind that it originates from an irreligious metal band. I read the statement in two senses: first, it says the only way to love is to embody God's love; and second, it says God is equivalent to love, so that to love is to know God and to know God is to know love. This latter premise echoes the teaching of 1 John 4, which says whoever loves knows God, and whoever does not love does not know God.

But what is love? There are many conceptions of love. It may be the most abused word in the English language. People often use the word to describe a feeling they have for someone or something. But love is not just a feeling. Love implies relationship, reciprocity, interconnectedness, and responsibility. Love is a verb. It exists in activity. As the theologian Thomas Jay Oord maintains, love implies intentional action toward the overall well-being of another.[7] To love is to concern yourself with another, to care for them and take responsibility for them. It is not just a giddy feeling inside when you think of someone.

At Union Theological Seminary, where I earned my master's of divinity, I would often hear quoted a saying from one of our professors, philosopher Cornel West: "Justice is what love looks like in public." This statement highlights the activity of love as care and concern for the wholeness of

6. This is precisely the mistake theologian John J. Johnson made. Rather than read Black Sabbath's theology on its own terms, Johnson compared Sabbath's verbiage with traditional Christian concepts and concluded that, in "After Forever," Sabbath confesses "an exclusivist view of salvation." His statement assumes a particular Christian soteriology, and thus misses Black Sabbath's creative engagement with Christian categories. See Johnson, "Christian Themes."

7. Oord, *Nature of Love*, 17.

others. If we love our neighbors, as Jesus called us to, we want justice, health, freedom, and peace for our neighbors. And if we understand every living thing as our neighbor, we can begin to understand the universality of God's love. God does not settle for sentimental feelings, but is actually concerned with *loving*. God is the only way to love because true love is concerned with the preservation of life and the pursuit of the common good.[8]

Love-come-to-life is the experience of God. Love is what saves us. It is God's conformity to love that makes God the salvation of life. Love sustains, nurtures life. Black Sabbath even says, "Love is life," in their song, "A National Acrobat." And in an interview when Bill Ward talked about religion, he said, "I believe in life and love."[9] Love saves us, because love is attentiveness to the survival, and care for the well-being, of life. The activity of *loving concern* is God's essence. God is the nurturer of life, defined by loving concern. God makes heaven real, not through escape to some other, happy world, but through love.

On "A National Acrobat," Ozzy also sings, "Love has given life to you, and now it's your concern." Love is a mother who gives birth to new life, and love itself is life. The life we have been given by love becomes the love that sustains us. This is Black Sabbath's theology of love. God is mother of all life, who nurtures and cares for every living thing.

So Sabbath's prophetic cry is a cry for love. Love is the demand of apocalyptic imagination and the answer to lament. In place of a world of oppression, where money is god, where the haves suppress the have-nots, where people

8. We can quote Dr. King again as well: "Love that does not satisfy justice is no love at all. It is merely a sentimental affection, little more than what one would have for a pet." King, *Where Do We Go from Here?*, 95.

9. "Black Sabbath Drummer Bill Ward Interviewed in 2010."

persecute those who are different from them—here, love screams and clamors a storm. Love created metal. Metal exists because Black Sabbath refused to substitute love for lesser evils. They made no peace with oppression.

In the end, Black Sabbath is not cynical or misanthropic. They do not reject the world as evil, but end up praising it as good. The world is good because the world is infused with love. "*Love is life*," and therefore life has its own intrinsic meaning and justification, an inherent goodness. This celebration of God's good creation comes to a zenith at the end of the album *Sabbath Bloody Sabbath*, in the song "Spiral Architect," to which we now turn.

It Is Good

The final song of *Sabbath Bloody Sabbath*, "Spiral Architect," is as epic and visionary a closer as any rock band could possibly hope for. It opens with Iommi playing classical guitar, then the band drives to a shimmering hard rock riff. By the time I hear Ozzy start to sing, "Sorcerers of madness / Selling me their time," I feel like Atreyu on the wings of Falkor, hovering in the skies above a world of darkness and deceit. Ozzy's vocal performance here is perhaps his greatest of all the Sabbath songs. There is such pain and longing in his voice, and the character of the vocal recording is positively surreal. This is not just a heavy metal song, it is not just a rock song, it transcends genre. It must have come out of the breath of Apollo himself. "Silver ships on plasmic oceans / In disguise."

In my estimation, "Spiral Architect" is also Geezer Butler's finest hour, his lyrical masterpiece. The title alone, which is never uttered in the song, evokes mystery and transcendence, and the poem seems itself like spiral architecture. The striking array of images that Geezer signals are beautiful yet head-spinning. In one minute, I know exactly what he means, but the next line comes and I am lost. Geezer even makes up his own words: "Synchronated undertaker"— "Metaphoric motories." You would be hard-pressed to find definitions of "synchronate" and "motory" in a dictionary, because they are not actual English words. It is as if the right words for what he was trying to say did not exist, and so he had to attempt his own.

Geezer said the song is about the way circumstances shape a particular human being. "Life's experiences," he explained, are "added to a person's DNA."[10] The frenzy of images in the song are like the forces which overdetermine human life: sorcerers, children of God, spiral skies, silver ships. Human existence is a deep black hole, a tossing to and fro. Ours is a world of contradictions.

> Child of God sitting in the sun
> Keeping peace of mind
> Fictional seduction
> On a black snow sky
> Sadness fills the superman
> Even fathers cry

The world does not move in a straight line, it spirals, through pain and uncertainty. Iommi captures the spiral in his guitar fills, his fingers tumbling down the fretboard. The song encapsulates all things in space and time, and dreams beyond them.

Time goes slow and yet is scarce. We only have a given time to our lives, yet we spend so much of it doing the bidding of sorcerers of madness. "Watching eyes of celluloid tell you how to live," we are under surveillance, so the powers can ensure we stay in line. "Separating sanity," "normal" is defined and enforced. We "give, give, give," of

10. Quoted in Black and Elliot, "Dark Knights Rise."

our energy, and we must *buy* time for ourselves. Human energy is transformed into mechanical energy—we are robotic code-followers.

But the chorus of "Spiral Architect," lifted by resplendent strings, points as if to a guiding star. Butler lists the things in life he values most of all: in the first chorus, "I look inside myself and see my world," in the second, "I see my memories," and in the last, "I look upon the earth." Over all three, Ozzy sings in knowing victory: "It is good."

The lyrics allude to the creation narrative in the book of Genesis: "God saw everything that he had made, and behold, it was very good" (Gen 1:31 ESV). But in Geezer's lyrics, there is a mutual fluency between God and the human being: "I look inside myself and see my world and know that it is good." The human subject claims the world for himself and himself deems it good. But this is no isolated subject. He invites the listener in: "You know that I should." The song ends repeating this last line. "You know that I should / You know that I should." You know the world is good. From God to me to you—we are all good. Love has given life to us, and now it's our concern.

Despite all the madness and confusion, the despotism and oppression, the world is good. Ozzy sings, "*Love is showing me the way.*" Love, that most persistent of four-letter words, is what makes the world good. Black Sabbath, the heavy metal, anti-flower-power band that made its name singing about war and Satan, still admits, like the Beatles, like the apostle Paul: love is the greatest thing, love is all you need.

Bibliography

Aarons, Ricky. "Geezer Butler—Heavy Metal Turns Fifty; The Birth of Black Sabbath." *Wall of Sound*, October 6, 2020.

Adorno, Theodor. *Negative Dialectics*. Translated by E. B. Ashton. New York: Continuum, 1973.

Alden, Robert L. "*Hoshek*." In *Theological Wordbook of the Old Testament*, edited by R. Laird Harris, 1:331. Chicago: Moody, 1980.

Alexander, Michelle. *The New Jim Crow: Mass Incarceration in the Age of Colorblindness*. Rev. ed. New York: New Press, 2012.

Alexandra, Rae. "The Insane World of Vintage Anti-Marijuana PSAs." *KQED*, December 4, 2017.

Alter, Robert. *Genesis: Translation and Commentary*. New York: Norton, 1996.

———. *The Wisdom Books: Job, Proverbs, and Ecclesiastes*. New York: Norton, 2010.

Arnett, Jeffrey. "Adolescents and Heavy Metal Music: From the Mouths of Metalheads." *Youth & Society* 23 (1991) 76–98.

———. *Metalheads: Heavy Metal Music and Adolescent Alienation*. New York: Routledge, 2018.

Aune, David E. *Revelation 1–5*. Dallas: Word, 1997.

Baraka, Amiri. *Blues People: Negro Music in White America*. New York: William Morrow, 1999.

Baldwin, James. *The Fire Next Time*. New York: Dial, 1963.

———. *No Name in the Street*. New York: Dial, 1972.

————. *The Price of the Ticket: Collected Nonfiction 1948–1985.* Boston: Beacon, 1985.

Banas, Erica. "Ozzy Osbourne Shows Support for Sharon Osbourne Following Exit from 'The Talk.'" *102.9 MGK*, April 1, 2021.

BangerTV. "Black Sabbath Drummer Bill Ward Interviewed in 2010 about the Band's Satanic Image." *YouTube*, August 25, 2016. https://www.youtube.com/watch?v=shHiUoqQbCQ.

Barnett, Brett A. "Black Sabbath's Pioneering Lyrical Rhetoric: Tragic Structure and Cathartic Potential in Song Narratives." *Metal Music Studies* 3 (2017) 81–96.

Barry, Colleen. "Climate Change Drives Venice Flooding, Even in Off-Season." *Associated Press*, October 20, 2021. https://www.mercurynews.com/2021/10/20/climate-change-drives-venice-flooding-even-in-off-season/.

Bauckham, Richard. *The Theology of the Book of Revelation.* Cambridge: Cambridge University Press, 1993.

Black, Johnny, and Paul Elliot. "The Dark Knights Rise: The Epic Story of Black Sabbath in the 70s." *Louder*, January 23, 2015.

Blaine, Jamie. "The Gospel according to Black Sabbath—a Conversation with Geezer Butler." *The Weeklings*, June 8, 2015. https://theweeklings.com/j-m-blaine/2015/06/08/geezer-butler.

Blight, David W. *Frederick Douglass: Prophet of Freedom.* New York: Simon & Schuster, 2018.

"The Blues." In *The Norton Anthology of African American Literature*, edited by Henry Louis Gate Jr. and Nellie Y. McKay, 48–49. 2nd ed. New York: Norton, 2004.

Boer, Roland. *Political Grace: The Revolutionary Theology of John Calvin.* Louisville: Westminster John Knox, 2009.

Bonhoeffer, Dietrich. *Letters & Papers from Prison.* Edited by John W. de Gruchy. Translated by Isabel Best et al. Minneapolis: Fortress, 2010.

Bowen, John. "Return of the Power Tool Killer." *Rue Morgue* 42 (2004) 16–22.

Brown, Elkisha. "Mammy Jars Mock Black People: Why Are They Still Collected?" *New York Times*, March 27, 2019.

Brueggemann, Walter. "The Costly Loss of Lament." *Journal of the Study of the Old Testament* 36 (1986) 57–71.

————. *The Prophetic Imagination.* 40th anniversary ed. Minneapolis: Fortress, 2018.

————. "The Shape of Old Testament Theology, II: Embrace of Pain." In *Old Testament Theology: Essays on Structure, Theme, and Text*, edited by Patrick D. Miller, 395–415. Minneapolis: Fortress, 1992.

Camus, Albert. *The Rebel*. Translated by Anthony Bower. New York: Knopf, 1954.

Canwell, Dianne, and Jon Sutherland. *African Americans in the Vietnam War*. Milwaukee: World Almanac Library, 2005.

Carey, Greg. "The Book of Revelation as Counter-Imperial Script." In *In The Shadow of Empire: Reclaiming the Bible as a History of Faithful Resistance*, edited by Richard Horsley, 157–76. Louisville: Westminster John Knox, 2008.

Carrington, Damian. "Climate Crisis: Scientists Spot Warning Signs of Gulf Stream Collapse." *Guardian*, August 5, 2021. https://www.theguardian.com/environment/2021/aug/05/climate-crisis-scientists-spot-warning-signs-of-gulf-stream-collapse.

Cave, Damien. "Great Barrier Reef Is Bleaching Again: It's Getting More Widespread." *New York Times*, April 6, 2020. https://www.nytimes.com/2020/04/06/world/australia/great-barrier-reefs-bleaching-dying.html.

Charlesworth, James H. *The Old Testament Pseudepigrapha*. 2 vols. Garden City: Doubleday, 1983.

Cleaver, Eldridge. *Soul on Ice*. New York: Dell, 1968.

Coates, Ta-Nehisi. *We Were Eight Years in Power: An American Tragedy*. New York: One World, 2018.

Collins, John J. *The Dead Sea Scrolls: A Biography*. Princeton: Princeton University Press, 2013.

Cone, James H. *A Black Theology of Liberation*. 40th anniversary ed. Maryknoll: Orbis, 2015.

———. *The Spirituals and the Blues*. Maryknoll: Orbis, 1972.

Conway, Kevin P., and Patrick McGrain. "Understanding Substance Use and Addiction through the Lyrics of Black Sabbath: A Content Analysis." *Substance Use & Misuse* 51 (2016) 1655–63.

Cope, Andrew L. "The Dichotomy of Aesthetics in Black Sabbath and Led Zeppelin." In *Black Sabbath and the Rise of Heavy Metal*, 71–94. London: Routledge, 2010.

Crowley, Aleister. *The Book of the Law*. Boston: Weiser, 1976.

Darnielle, John. *Master of Reality*. London: Bloomsbury, 2008.

Davis, Angela Y. *Blues Legacies and Black Feminism: Gertrude "Ma" Rainey, Bessie Smith, and Billie Holiday*. New York: Pantheon, 1998.

Day, Peggy L. *An Adversary in Heaven: Satan in the Hebrew Bible*. Atlanta: Scholars, 1988.

Douglass, Frederick. *Narrative of the Life of Frederick Douglass*. New Haven, CT: Yale University Press, 2016.

Ellington, Scott A. *Risking Truth: Reshaping the World through Prayers of Lament*. Eugene, OR: Pickwick, 2008.

European Monitoring Centre for Drugs and Drug Addiction (EMCDDA). "Medical Use of Cannabis and Cannabinoids: Questions and Answers for Policymaking." European Monitoring Centre for Drugs and Drug Addiction. December 2018. https://www.emcdda.europa.eu/publications/rapid-communications/medical-use-of-cannabis-and-cannabinoids-questions-and-answers-for-policymaking_en.

Fanon, Frantz. *Black Skin, White Masks*. Translated by Charles Lam Markmann. London: Pluto, 1967.

————. *The Wretched of the Earth*. Translated by Constance Farrington. New York: Grove, 1963.

Farley, Helen. "Demons, Devils, and Witches." In *Heavy Metal Music in Britain*, edited by Gerd Bayer, 73–88. London: Routledge, 2016.

Feuerbach, Ludwig. *The Essence of Christianity*. Translated by George Eliot. New York: Harper Torchbooks, 1957.

Foucault, Michel. *Discipline and Punish: The Birth of the Prison*. 2nd ed. New York: Vintage, 1995.

Froese, Brian. "'Is It the End, My Friend?' Black Sabbath's Apocalypse of Horror." In *Black Sabbath and Philosophy*, edited by William Irvin, 20–30. Malden, MA: Wiley-Blackwell, 2013.

Gebara, Ivone. "The Face of Transcendence as a Challenge to the Reading of the Bible in Latin America." In *Searching the Scriptures: A Feminist Introduction*, edited by Elisabeth Schüssler Fiorenza, 1:172–85. New York: Crossroad, 1993.

Glaude, Eddie S., Jr. *Begin Again: James Baldwin's America and Its Urgent Lessons for Our Own*. New York: Crown, 2020.

Goldman, Albert. "Why Do Whites Sing Black?" *New York Times*, December 14, 1969.

Gussow, Adam. *Beyond the Crossroads: The Devil and the Blues Tradition*. Chapel Hill: University of North Carolina Press, 2017.

Hamilton, Jack. *Just Around Midnight: Rock and Roll and the Racial Imagination*. Cambridge, MA: Harvard University Press, 2016.

Hanson, Paul D. "Apocalypse and Apocalypticism: The Genre." In *The Anchor Bible Dictionary*, edited by David Noel Freedman, 1:279–92. New York: Doubleday, 1992.

Harmon, Justin. "The Crossroads: Selling Your Soul for Rock n' Roll." *Leisure Sciences* 43 (2020) 606.

Harris, R. Laird. "She'ol." In *Theological Wordbook of the Old Testament*, edited by Harris et al., 2:892. Chicago: Moody, 1980.

Harrison, Leigh Michael. "Factory Music: How the Industrial Geography and Working-Class Environment of Post-War Birmingham Fostered the Birth of Heavy Metal." *Journal of Social History* 44 (2010) 145–58.

HDBlackSabbath. "Black Sabbath—Live at the Audimax, Berlin, West Germany (1970) (Source 2)." *YouTube*, January 26, 2020. https://www.youtube.com/watch?v=lDWplsgZG7E&t=1075s.

Heiser, Michael S. "The Mythological Provenance of Isa. XIV 12–15: A Reconsideration of the Ugaritic Material." *Vetus Testamentum* 51 (2001) 354–69.

The Hellfire God. "Black Sabbath—Walpurgis Remastered 1970 HQ." *YouTube*, December 11, 2015. https://www.youtube.com/watch?v=20rnmR4awug.

Heschel, Abraham Joshua. *The Prophets*. New York: Harper & Row, 1962.

Home of Metal. "Geezer Butler Talks about His Religious Upbringing." *YouTube*, May 21, 2019. https://www.youtube.com/watch?v=1F9HDrf4zs4.

Horsley, Richard A. "Jesus and Empire." In *The Shadow of Empire: Reclaiming the Bible as a History of Faithful Resistance*, 75–96. Louisville: Westminster John Knox, 2008.

Hoskyns, Barney. *Into the Void: Ozzy Osbourne and Black Sabbath*. London: Omnibus, 2004.

Iommi, Tony, with T. J. Lammers. *Iron Man: My Journey through Heaven & Hell with Black Sabbath*. Boston: Da Capo, 2011.

Johnson, John J. "Christian Themes in the Heavy Metal Music of Black Sabbath?" *Implicit Religion* 17 (2014) 321–35.

Katz, Mark. *Capturing Sound: How Technology Has Changed Music*. Rev. ed. Berkeley: University of California Press, 2010.

Kawabata, Maiko. "Virtuosity, the Violin, the Devil . . . What *Really* Made Paganini 'Demonic'?" *Current Musicology* 83 (2007) 85–108.

Kelly, Emma. "Sharon Osbourne Apologises for Offending Black Community after Emotional Defence of Piers Morgan." *Metro*, March 12, 2021.

Kelly, Kim. "Inside Heavy Metal's Battle against White Supremacy." *Esquire*, November 12, 2020. https://www.esquire.com/entertainment/music/a34633291/heavy-metal-nazi-anti-fascist-movement/.

Kendi, Ibram X. *Stamped from the Beginning: The Definitive History of Racist Ideas in America*. New York: Bold Type, 2016.

King, Martin Luther, Jr. *Where Do We Go from Here—Chaos or Community?* Boston: Beacon, 1968.

Knowles, Elizabeth, ed. *The Oxford Dictionary of Phrase and Fable (ODPF)*. 2nd ed. Oxford: Oxford University Press, 2005.

Kopkind, Andrew. "They'd Rather Be Left." *New York Review of Books*, September 28, 1967. https://www.nybooks.com/articles/1967/09/28/theyd-rather-be-left/.

Kubik, Gerhard. *Africa and the Blues*. University Press of Mississippi, 1999.

Kwai, Isabella. "U.N. Reclassifies Cannabis as a Less Dangerous Drug." *New York Times*, December 2, 2020.

Lawrence, Mark Atwood. *The Vietnam War: A Concise International History*. Oxford: Oxford University Press, 2008.

Littmann, Greg. "The Art of Black Sabbath: Aristotle Joins the Band." In *Black Sabbath & Philosophy: Mastering Reality*, edited by William Irwin, 63–75. West Sussex, UK: Wiley-Blackwell, 2013.

Longe, Jacqueline L. *Gale Encyclopedia of Psychology (GEP)*. 3rd ed. Detroit: Gale, 2016.

Lorde, Audre. "Learning from the 60s." In *Sister Outsider*, 134–44. Berkeley, CA: Crossing, 2007.

Mahon, Maureen. *Right to Rock: The Black Rock Coalition and the Cultural Politics of Race*. Durham, NC: Duke University Press, 2004.

Maier, Harry O. *New Testament Christianity in the Roman World*. Oxford: Oxford University Press, 2019.

Malcolm X. *The Autobiography of Malcolm X*. With Alex Haley. New York: Ballantine, 1964.

————. Speech at Nation of Islam Temple No. 15. Atlanta, 1960. Recording retrieved from Columbia Center for New Media Teaching and Learning. https://ccnmtl.columbia.edu/projects/mmt/mxp/speeches/mxa10.html.

Marwick, Arthur. *The Sixties: Cultural Revolution in Britain, France, Italy, and the United States, c. 1958–1974*. Oxford: Oxford University Press, 1998.

Marx, Karl. *Contribution to the Critique of Hegel's Philosophy of Law*. Translated by Jack Cohen. Marx and Engels Collected Works 3. New York: International, 1975.

McKay, George. *Circular Breathing: The Cultural Politics of Jazz in Britain*. Durham, NC: Duke University Press, 2005.

Moore, Ryan M. "The Unmaking of the English Working Class: Deindustrialization, Reification and the Origins of Heavy Metal." In *Heavy Metal Music in Britain*, edited by Gerd Bayer, 143–60. London: Routledge, 2016.

Newton, Steve. "Judas Priest's Rob Halford Calls 'Black Sabbath' the Most Evil Song That's Ever Been Written." *Ear of Newt*, October 10, 2015. https://earofnewt.com/2015/10/01/judas-priests-rob-halford-calls-black-sabbath-the-most-evil-song-thats-ever-been-written/.

Niermann, Matthew. *The Humble Creative*. Eugene, OR: Wipf & Stock, 2021.

Nietzsche, Friedrich. *The Birth of Tragedy*. Translated by Ronald Speirs. Cambridge: Cambridge University Press, 1999.

———. *The Genealogy of Morals*. Translated by Horace B. Samuel. Mineola, NY: Dover, 2003.

Oakley, Giles. *The Devil's Music: A History of the Blues*. 2nd ed. Boston: Da Capo, 1997.

Oord, Thomas Jay. *The Nature of Love: A Theology*. St. Louis: Chalice, 2010.

Osbourne, Ozzy. *I Am Ozzy*. With Chris Ayres. New York: Grand Central, 2009.

Osbourne, Sharon. *Extreme: My Autobiography*. London: Time Warner, 2005.

Payne, Les, and Tamara Payne. *The Dead Are Arising: The Life of Malcolm X*. New York: Norton, 2020.

Pearson, Barry Lee, and Bill McCulloch. *Robert Johnson: Lost and Found*. Urbana: University of Illinois Press, 2003.

Polcaro, Rafael. "Sabbath's Geezer Butler Explains the Origins of His Nickname 'Geezer.'" *Rock and Roll Garage*, July 21, 2019. http://rockandrollgarage.com/sabbaths-geezer-butler-explains-the-origin-of-his-nickname-geezer/.

Ranbsy, Barbara. "The White Left Needs to Embrace Black Leadership." *The Nation*, July 2, 2020.

Rare Metal Videos. "Rare Ozzy Osbourne Video—USA 1981 TV Interview 2 on the Town." *YouTube*, October 25, 2013. https://www.youtube.com/watch?v=Q_POnE9muos&t=332s.

ReelinInTheYears66. "Black Sabbath—Interview 1973." *YouTube*, December 4, 2018. https://www.youtube.com/watch?v=vX6NAJWUep8.

Reesman, Bryan. "Geezer Butler Discusses Veganism, Religion, Politics, Surveillance, and Life Lessons." *Attention Deficit Delirium*, March 27, 2014. https://www.bryanreesman.com/2014/03/27/

geezer-butler-discusses-veganism-religion-politics
-surveillance-and-life-lessons/.

Robinson, Cedric L. *Black Marxism: The Making of the Black Radical Tradition.* 3rd ed. Chapel Hill: University of North Carolina Press, 1983.

Roper, Lyndal. *Witch Craze: Terror and Fantasy in Baroque Germany.* New Haven, CT: Yale University Press, 2004.

Rosen, Steven. *Wheels of Confusion: The Story of Black Sabbath.* Chessington, UK: Castle Communications, 1996.

Rossinow, Douglas C. *The Politics of Authenticity: Liberalism, Christianity, and the New Left in America.* New York: Columbia University Press, 1998.

Rubenstein, Steve, and Michael Cabanatuan. "Bay Area Transfixed by Foreboding, Orange, Smoke-Choked Skies." *San Francisco Chronicle,* September 9, 2020. https://www.sfchronicle.com/bayarea/article/Bay-Area-awakes-to-foreboding-smoke-choked-15553731.php.

Ruether, Rosemary Radford. *Sexism and God-Talk: Toward a Feminist Theology.* Boston: Beacon, 1993.

Schüssler Fiorenza, Elisabeth. *The Book of Revelation: Justice and Judgment.* 2nd ed. Minneapolis: Fortress, 1998.

Sharma, Amit. "Geezer Butler: Heavy Metal Keeps You Going . . . I Still Feel Like I'm 25!" *Kerrang,* July 17, 2019. https://www.kerrang.com/features/geezer-butler-heavy-metal-keeps-you-young-i-still-feel-like-im-25/.

Sharman, Leah, and Genevieve Anita Dingle. "Extreme Metal Music and Anger Processing." *Frontiers in Human Neuroscience* 9 (2015) 1–11.

Sonderegger, Katherine. *Systematic Theology.* Vol. 1, *The Doctrine of God.* Minneapolis: Fortress, 2015.

Stolz, Nolan. *Experiencing Black Sabbath: A Listener's Companion.* Lanham, MD: Rowman & Littlefield, 2017.

Taibbi, Matt. *The Divide: American Injustice in the Age of the Wealth Gap.* New York: Spiegel & Grau, 2014.

Tracy, Emmett P. "Hendrix, Jimi." In *The Encyclopedia of African American History, 1896 to the Present,* edited by Paul Finkelman, 2:409–10. Oxford: Oxford University Press, 2009.

Tupman, Tracy W. "Theatre Magick: Aleister Crowley and the Rites of Eleusis." PhD diss., Ohio State University, 2003.

Vermes, Geza. *The Complete Dead Sea Scrolls in English.* New York: Penguin, 2011.

Vulliamy, Graham. "The Roots of Black Music." In *Jazz & Blues*, 6–26. London: Routledge, 1982.

Wall, Mick. *Black Sabbath: Symptom of the Universe*. New York: St. Martin's, 2013.

Walser, Robert. *Running with the Devil: Power, Gender, and Madness in Heavy Metal Music*. Middletown, CT: Wesleyan University Press, 2014.

Ward, Bill. "Black Sabbath Drummer Bill Ward Looks Back at the Band's Rise to Heavy Metal Glory." *New York Daily News*, June 1, 2010.

Ward, Brian. *Just My Soul Responding: Rhythm and Blues, Black Consciousness, and Race Relations*. London: Routledge, 2012.

Weinstein, Deena. *Heavy Metal: A Cultural Sociology*. New York: Lexington, 1991.

Werner, Craig. *A Change Is Gonna Come: Music, Race & the Soul of America*. Ann Arbor: University of Michigan Press, 2006.

Williams, Michael, and Catherine Marfin. "QAnon Supporters Gather Downtown Dallas Expecting JFK Jr." *Dallas News*, November 2, 2021.

Wray, T. J., and Gregory Mobley. *The Birth of Satan: Tracing the Devil's Biblical Roots*. New York: St. Martin's, 2005.